Also by David Owen

High School
None of the Above
The Man Who Invented Saturday Morning
The Walls Around Us
My Usual Game
Lure of the Links (coeditor)
Around the House
(also published as *Life Under a Leaky Roof*)
The Making of the Masters
The Chosen One
The First National Bank of Dad
Copies in Seconds

HIT
&
HOPE

How the Rest of Us Play Golf

DAVID OWEN

SIMON & SCHUSTER PAPERBACKS
NEW YORK   LONDON   TORONTO   SYDNEY

SIMON & SCHUSTER PAPERBACKS
Rockefeller Center
1230 Avenue of the Americas
New York, NY 10020

First Simon & Schuster paperback edition 2005

SIMON & SCHUSTER PAPERBACKS and colophon are registered
trademarks of Simon & Schuster, Inc.

For information about special discounts for bulk purchases,
please contact Simon & Schuster Special Sales:
1-800-456-6798 or business@simonandschuster.com

Designed by Jan Pisciotta

Manufactured in the United States of America

1   3   5   7   9   10   8   6   4   2

The Library of Congress has cataloged the hardcover edition as follows:
Owen, David
Hit and hope : how the rest of us play golf / David Owen
p. cm
1. Golf—Anecdotes. I. Title.GV967.096 2003
796.352—dc21   2003041564

ISBN 0-7432-2237-7
0-7432-6146-1 (pbk)

For Bob Witkoski, Fran Hoxie,
and Zane Chappy,
and in memory of Dave Johnson

Golf is the thing with feathers—
That perches on the soul—
And sings the tune without the words—
And never stops—at all—

I've heard it in the chillest land—
and on the strangest Sea—
Yet, never, in Extremity,
It asked a crumb—of Me.

EMILY DICKINSON

HIT
&
*H*OPE

Hit & Hope

An Introduction

Hᴏɪᴛ ᴀ ɢᴏʟꜰ ʙᴀʟʟ ᴡᴇʟʟ and every neuron in your body yearns to duplicate the experience. Like kissing, it's a pleasure that repetition can't diminish. I remember my first good golf shot—a four-iron that somehow soared two hundred yards down the middle of a gently left-bending fairway— as though I hit it last week. The shot was a fluke, of course, but it made a visceral impression. That's it, I thought immediately; give me another one of those.

I discovered golf on the front step of middle age: I was thirty-six years old when a friend, on a whim, invited me to play, and I, on a whim, went. Although I hate to admit it, I measure my life as a mature person from that moment. Most of my best friends now are people I play golf with. Most of what I do for a living is connected in some way to golf. Most of the presents I receive are golf-related. Most of my clothes are golf clothes, most of my trips are golf trips, most of my dreams are golf dreams. Almost all of my remaining ambitions involve my swing.

The essays that make up this book were written mainly for *Golf Digest*, to which I have contributed a monthly column since 1996. I've fiddled with almost all of these pieces, and, in some cases, I've restored material that had to be cut to accommodate the modest dimensions of my corner in the front of the magazine. I've also combined a few related essays, extended others, written a number of new ones, and resurrected (from two previous books of mine) a couple of short bits that I wanted to keep in print. All of these essays arose from whatever happened to be going on with my golf game at the moment I wrote them. I've tried to arrange them in a plausible order, but, in truth, they are fragments, not chapters, and they should be read in the same way that I hit practice balls: quickly, randomly, and with a short attention span.

Sweet Sunday Morning

MY REGULAR SUNDAY-MORNING golf group begins to gather a little before seven-thirty. If there's frost on the course, we stand around drinking coffee until my friend Ray, who is the head of the greens committee, announces that the ice on the grass is "just dew." Anyone who shows up is welcome to play; we seldom have fewer than a dozen, and we sometimes have more than twenty. We choose teams by drawing numbered poker chips from someone's hat, and if the total isn't divisible by four we send some of the players out in threesomes. The threesomes begin two strokes under par—an adjustment we borrowed from Augusta National, where the members' weekend games are known, definitively, as "the Games." Our pro, whose name is Fran, plays with us when he can find someone to cover for him in the golf shop. Our superintendent, whose name is Bob, plays with us when we can cajole him into dragging his clubs from the back of his garage, where he also keeps a thirty-year-old Corvette and a beer-stocked refrigerator that we are allowed to pilfer in emergencies.

We have our own scorecard, which my friend Jim created with a desktop-publishing program. Jim's scorecard allocates handicap strokes in the order in which we want them to be allocated, and it depicts the course the way we like to play it, with four way-back tees that almost nobody else ever uses. There are no red tees on the card. On the back is a list of nine local rules, which apply only to our competition. One of the rules was inspired by a player we call Uncle Frank: "No competitor shall dress in a black-and-white sun suit purchased by his wife." Three regular members of the group—Harry, Gene, and George—are no longer allowed to keep score, because each of them once made a computation error that led to a tedious discussion and a redistribution of winnings. The card also lists our Sunday-morning course record, which is nine over par, net—a score that is almost inconceivably bad, considering that nine *under* par is seldom good enough to win. The course record was set on October 22, 2001, by Frank (not Uncle Frank), Rick, and me.

We bet, obviously. My friend Hacker (yes, that's his real last name) collects all the money before we tee off and keeps it in his wallet while we play; semi-miraculously, he has never come up short. The mandatory wager is twelve dollars: five goes into a pool for the winning team, five goes into a pool for skins, and two goes into a pot that is shared by everyone who matches the morning's best net score on the so-called Money Hole, which we pick at random before we tee off by drawing another numbered poker chip from another hat. On the day that Rick, Frank, and I set the course record, we actually would have been ten over par if I hadn't birdied the final hole, which happened to be the Money Hole; my birdie was unmatched by anyone else, so it entitled me to the entire Money Hole pot plus a skin, meaning that I won more money—forty-two dollars—than anyone else that day, despite having helped to turn in the worst team score in recorded history.

The game is net best ball, first-tee do-over, no junk, no gimmes, summer rules unless previously agreed. We play off the lowest handicap, but nobody gets more than one stroke a hole and nobody strokes on a par-three. If you wear shorts after November 1, you get one additional handicap stroke, but you have to keep your shorts on for the whole round, and you can't wear rain pants on top of them. Over the course of a season, almost everyone plays with almost everyone else, so yippers, shankers, and creative self-handicappers are not treated as pariahs. Whether or not our pro should have a handicap is an endlessly fascinating topic of debate; at the moment, we call Fran a zero.

When we have finished, we drink beer and cook hamburgers on the patio between the clubhouse and the practice green. (Our clubhouse, which looks like an Adirondack cabin and used to be a prep-school fraternity house, doesn't have a restaurant or a grill room, thank God.) One of the chairs on the patio is reserved for Bob; there is an old blue-and-white enameled metal sign on the back of his seat that says SUPER-

INTENDENT, and there is a bottle opener screwed onto one of its arms. We take turns supplying lunch, about which there are three rules: no plates, no napkins, and no salad. If there are potato chips, we eat them out of the bag. If nobody remembers to bring lunch, somebody runs into town and buys supplies before the grocery store closes, at one o'clock. The first group to finish fires up the grill. Bob sometimes contributes a pound or two of ground venison, from a deer he shot the winter before in the woods that surround our golf course. Bob's wife, Diane, usually seasons the venison, shapes it into patties, wraps the patties in aluminum foil, and leaves the package for us on the top shelf of the refrigerator in the clubhouse kitchen while we're playing. Hers are the only female hands that have ever touched our lunch.

Often, our games end in ties. Matching cards would be boring, and playing extra holes would force the participants to travel too far from the beer coolers,* so we almost always conduct our playoffs on or around the practice green. If someone earns a skin but doesn't stick around for the shouting match at which we distribute the money, we conduct a playoff for his skin money, too. On various occasions, we have required play-

---

* A reader named John Creque, from Pinehurst, North Carolina, wrote to say that he and his golf buddies had solved this problem, by inventing a side competition called "cooler golf," which they play alongside their regular nassau. Cooler golf has many, many rules, as all good golf games do, but the basic idea is that the player who has the worst score on a hole is required to carry the foursome's entire beer supply until somebody else does worse: "The laggard lugs the lager."

off contestants to: putt balls from the top of a beer can while standing on the seat of a chair on the patio; throw balls from the big tree next to the first tee; throw balls onto the roof of the clubhouse so that they roll down the porch roof, down the porch steps, across the patio, and down the short, steep grassy slope above the practice green; chip balls through the split-rail fence that separates the patio from the parking lot; and lob balls from the pinnacle of a four-foot-tall pile of dirt in the middle of the first tee, which was being rebuilt. In all our play-offs, we use the stymie rule, which the rest of the golf world abandoned in 1953: your ball stays where it stops, even if it's blocking someone else's putt. When we have large groups, we sometimes save time by making everyone putt at the same time, toward a single hole. Once, in pouring rain, we conducted a playoff inside the clubhouse, with a long putt that had to run from the (linoleum) floor of the kitchen all the way across the (carpeted) floor of the living room. The target was a beer bottle.

One Sunday a couple of years ago, two foursomes tied for the lead in our morning competition, and the playoff committee decided, for the first time, to venture beyond the clubhouse and the practice green. The playoff, they declared, would be the eighteenth hole, alternate shot, sandwedges only. Our eighteenth is a short par-four under ordinary circumstances, but playing it with just a sand-wedge turns it into a grueling par-five. The tee shot is nerve-wracking, because the carry to the fairway is close to eighty yards. On this particular Sunday, though, the battle came down to the green. A friend, whom I'll call Mr. Yips, had to use his sand wedge (a club he hates) to attempt a two-foot putt (a shot that gives him nightmares) for the win. I can't bear to describe exactly what happened, but I will say that by the time it was over people were laughing so hard they could scarcely stand up, and somebody had to rake the bunker on the far side of the green.

Sometimes, a playoff format seems like so much fun that we open it to the whole group, including caddies. Other players, getting ready to tee off on the first hole, invariably scowl when they see us standing in a long row with our backs to the practice green, holding a beer in one hand and weighing a ball in the other, getting ready to throw the ball over a shoulder at one of the holes, and quietly dreading the moment when, finally, it will be time to go home.

You Must Remember This

I RECENTLY WATCHED, for the twentieth or thirtieth time, the best golf movie ever made. Not *Caddyshack*, although I'm a fan. And not *Tin Cup*, in which Kevin Costner swings like a chicken and tucks his sweater into his pants. And not *Follow the Sun*, in which Glenn Ford makes you believe that Ernest Borgnine (for example) would have made a better Ben Hogan. And definitely not *Bagger Vance*.

No, the all-time No. 1 golf movie was made in 1942 by Michael Curtiz. It's set in Morocco, and it stars Humphrey Bogart and Claude Rains. Ingrid Bergman is in it, too. It's called *Casablanca*. Have you heard of it?

Casablanca isn't only about golf. There's a long boring part at the beginning in which the Nazis make a lot of trouble, and various people sing various songs in Bogart's nightclub, and Bogart apparently has some sort of love affair with Bergman—although you never actually see them doing anything except talking to each other with their faces a quarter-inch apart. This boring stretch lasts for about an hour and a half. I usually let my wife watch it by herself, while I make popcorn or take the dogs for a walk.

The golf part comes near the end. Bogart and Bergman and a wimpy-looking foreign guy, who appears to be wearing lipstick, turn up at a foggy airport one night, and for a moment you think that Bergman is going to dump the lipstick guy and marry Bogart. That's the suspense. Bergman is good-looking, despite the hat, but you can tell that as soon as the wedding is over she's going to start demanding lifestyle changes, and the first thing to go will be the nightclub. Then she'll say, "Oh, Rick, do we really need to live in Africa?" Then they'll have four kids in a hurry, and that will be that.

But Bogart sees the trap a mile away. He makes Bergman think he's going along with her scheme, but at the last second he tricks her into getting on the plane. "You're taking the fall," he says to the lipstick guy. (I'm paraphrasing now.) Then the plane heads down the runway—whew!—and Bogart and Rains escape into the fog, so that they can spend the rest of World War Two drinking gin and playing golf. I tell you, that movie makes me cry every time.

Causation

I LIKE TO USE FOREIGN COINS to mark my golf balls. In my bag I have Russian kopecks, Moroccan dirhams, Mexican pesos, Aruban florins, Slovenian stotins, and so many British coins of all denominations that I could just about cover the cost of a trip to the Open. I also have a reproduction of an ancient Roman coin, some old tokens from the subway systems of Boston and New York, half a dozen game tokens from Discovery Zone and Rollermagic, and a squashed, elongated American penny embossed with the Lord's Prayer.

My best ball marker, though, is an Irish twenty-pence piece. It's brassy looking and slightly wider and thicker than a Susan B. Anthony dollar. There's a horse on one side and a harp on the other, and if I point the nose of the horse at my ball when I mark it, the next putt will go in or come very, very close. To make the horse work, I have to keep the coin in my pocket with three or four others and pull it out by accident. Recently, I've also had encouraging results with a Canadian looney.

As for boxers or briefs, I can't really say; I've won while wearing both. Going beltless didn't work the one time I did it (not on purpose). The more important the match, the less important-looking the golf shirt ought to be, I've found. My Meat Loaf hat—a regular golf hat autographed by the recording artist—used to guarantee victory but is now worthless; I never wear it anymore, even around the house. Which socks I put on, to be perfectly frank, doesn't seem to make much of a difference.

Non-golfers may dismiss a reliance on Meat Loaf hats and lucky underpants as superstition. But superstition is a vestige of the most important moment in human evolution: the rise of conceptual thought. You try something, and something else happens—a pattern emerges. That's how our ancestors came up with fire, the Renaissance, and the rest. And that's how I came up with Irish coins—which, at this point, are probably the most dependable part of my game.

Forgetting to carry one old ball in a rear pants pocket can cause a tee shot to slice out of bounds. Reusing an unbroken tee from which an opponent has just hit a bad drive will usually guarantee a good shot. The best way to warm up before a match is to hit balls with a club that won't be needed on the course. Being wished good luck upon leaving the house is practically fatal. New clubs work better if bought without being tried. Never retire a ball that has just made a birdie. Always be sure that the last practice putt before teeing off is a miss.

The Slowest Member

THE SLOWEST MEMBER OF MY CLUB has the metabolism of a sofa. Standing over his golf ball, he freezes like a frog in a flashlight beam. Five seconds. Ten seconds. An afternoon. Just when you think he must have drifted into sleep, he swings—but it's a practice swing, the first of two. Each rehearsal spawns a divot. Each divot flies in its own direction. At last, he inches forward and sets his club behind the ball.

Thirty minutes a hole is the pace at which he plays. He moves through our nine-hole course the way a meal moves through a python. You could tee off an hour behind him and play through him twice before he reached the ninth tee. He is absorbed by his troubles and seldom notices other golfers. You are tempted to wait for him to wander into the bushes, then tee off over his head.

The Slowest Member lifts his five-iron as wearily as if it were the hammer of Thor. He pauses at shoulder height to gather his resources, then lunges forward while somehow also falling back. His ball flies forty yards ahead and thirty to the right, and it doesn't rise above his navel. He slowly lifts his head and looks around. The destination of each shot is first a mystery and then a surprise.

Once, I saw him walk into some pine trees to search for a ball that he had hit there. He didn't take a club. After a minute or so, his wife hissed at him from the green, which he had missed from twenty paces. Golfers in the fairway took furious practice swings, hoping to be waved through. His wife hissed again. Her impatience merely inflamed his determination not to hurry. If his ball had been your child, you would have given up sooner than he did.

Some years, the Slowest Member plays more rounds than anyone else at my club. Each weekend gapes before him, an empty barrel to be filled one pebble at a time. The rest of us scan the parking lot when we pull in. Is he here yet? When did he tee off? One day, I saw his foursome spaced along the near shore of the pond on the fourth hole, each player with a ball retriever. Trolling the murky waters, happily lost in thought, they looked like fishermen.

In a two-day tournament one summer, the Slowest Member was the only entrant in his flight. His name on a sign-up sheet is preemptive. "Give him the title by default," someone suggested. "Tell him he can have the cup if he stays home." Even alone, he moves more slowly than any foursome except his own.

In the end, a playing partner was drafted from a different flight. Their twosome teed off last. The Slowest Member sliced two drives out of bounds before dribbling a keeper over the end of the first tee. The playing partner sighed, his own drive now grown cold in the fairway, a thousand miles away. "At least we're off," he must have thought.

But they weren't off, after all. The Slowest Member walked right past his ball. Moving at the speed of the minute hand on a classroom clock, he set out for the woods to look for the two that he had lost.

Shagging Your Own

AT THE DRIVING RANGE at my club, golf balls are promiscuously available. There's a big steel bin, like a junior Dumpster, and we can help ourselves. The balls don't pop up automatically on rubber tees, the way they do at those triple-decker driving ranges in Japan, but they might as well. Some golfers scarcely look up between shots. As soon as one ball is gone, they toe another into place.

I often do the same thing myself. When my swing turns sour, I attempt a frantic intervention, churning through two or three buckets in the desperate hope that at some point quantity will tip the balance into quality, and my hook or shank or slice will admit defeat and go away. Before we got the bin, you could hit balls only when the pro was around to dole them out one bag at a time. Now, we all practice more. But do we practice better?

Not too many years ago, there were no range balls at my club. In fact, there was no range. Golfers who wanted to practice had to use their own balls, and they had to hit them across two fairways to a narrow field that slicers on the sixth tee treated as an optional landing area. Concern for the skulls of fellow members promoted compact swings and careful attention to fundamentals. You can still see a few of the old-timers' shag bags hanging among the rafters in the bag room. The balls inside them are so old and brown they seem like golf-ball fossils.

During the shoulder season at my club—the weeks in early spring and late fall when the range is open but the bin is locked—we still hit balls the old-fashioned way, those few of us who don't mind shagging our own. I have a collection of practice balls which I have built over several seasons. There are balls that I have fished out of ponds and pried out of the ground, balls that I have bounced off stone walls or gouged with my five-iron, balls that I have found in peculiar places, such as underneath a soda machine at a rest stop on I-84. Exposure to the sun has made some of them softer than blackboard chalk. Their worn corporate logos are as familiar as faces in a yearbook. I keep them all in a bucket beside my back door. When the bucket is more than half-full, I feel rich; if it dips below half-empty, I feel poor. During the season, I knock the balls around my yard. In early spring and late fall, I take them to the range.

You spend more time on a practice shot if you own the ball. You aim at something small, check your grip, and take a practice swing. You look at your target again. You visualize the shape of the shot. Because you have to pick up after yourself, you think about ways to tighten your landing pattern. Because you pace the yardage as you walk to retrieve your balls, you learn how far your eight-iron really goes. You learn what the wind does to your shots, and what it doesn't do. You have time to think about what you are up to.

In a crudely mown field in England once, I watched a gray-haired golfer collect three dozen or four dozen balls, which he had spent the previous hour hitting. He walked in a loose spiral around his target, using a wedge to flip each ball into an open bowling bag, which he held in his other hand. He never bent over. He seldom dropped a ball. There was a rhythm to what he was doing, and that rhythm, you got the feeling, was the backbone of his game. I tried the same flip later, and couldn't pull it off. In another generation or two, will there be anyone who can?

The Horrifying
Popularity of Golf

IT WAS MASTERS WEEK of 1997 when I first sensed something was wrong. I called home from Augusta to check in with my family, and my wife said, "That was some eight-iron Tiger hit into thirteen today. But don't you think Fluff should have taken the driver out of his hands on three?"

I quickly asked her what my sister's husband had given me for Christmas. She knew the answer—he gave me nothing. So she really was my wife. But what was going on? Before that moment, our conversations about golf had mainly concerned her hypothesis that I am a bad person because I play it. Now, all of a sudden, she was worried about club selection.

I used to lie, even to myself, about how much golf I play. Now, strangers at cocktail parties are interested in what I shot. "Have you met Tiger?" a checker at the grocery store asked one day after noticing that my left hand was less tanned than my right—evidence that I had been wearing a golf glove. My home course is suddenly clogged with people who putt with the flag in the hole and don't know what a press is.

One afternoon a few months after Tiger's victory in Augusta, my son and I went to the driving range to escape trouble at home. (My wife was helping our daughter and two of her friends get ready for the seventh-grade semi-formal. My son and I were cowering in the kitchen, when he suddenly turned to me and said, "Hit some balls?") I hadn't been to the range in quite a while, because my new theory of the golf swing, *pace* Hogan, is that every day you spend practicing means one more day until you get better. So I was unprepared for what I found: Every parking space was filled, and every plastic mat was occupied. "It's been like this since the Masters," a Sunday-morning buddy of mine muttered glumly as he kicked the dirt near his car.

Tiger got us into this mess, and only Tiger can get us out. He needs to be a man and do for golf what the players' strike did for baseball. It won't be much of a sacrifice for him; he's already had what most pros would consider a fabulous career. Here's what he has to do:

- Switch to tennis.
- Spearhead a "Just Say No to Golf" campaign for beginning players.
- Announce the formation of a company to build 72-hole golf resorts in South American rain forests.
- Run for president. (Either the national press will destroy him, or he'll be elected and have no time to play).

The danger, of course, is that these measures will backfire, and people who used to complain about pesticides on golf courses will decide that deforesting Brazil would be a good idea. If that happens, I'm afraid we're going to have to do something really drastic. We're going to have to go back to wearing plaid polyester pants and three-inch-wide white-vinyl belts.

Feelings

"YOU WOULD HAVE BEEN PROUD OF ME, DEAR," I told my wife after returning from a weeklong golf trip to Florida with three of my friends. "One day, while we were waiting for a slow group to clear the green ahead of us, I asked Tom what he does for a living."

My wife is appalled that my golf buddies and I never talk about anything except drivers, putters, theories of the golf swing, Stimpmeter readings, and whose turn it is to pay for the beer. She thinks we ought to spend at least some of our time doing what she and her friends spend almost all of their time doing: sharing "feelings." She also thinks we are barbarically uncurious about one another's personal lives. Sample conversation:

My wife: "You and Jim have played golf every Sunday for years. Wouldn't you like to invite him and his wife to dinner?"

Me: "Jim is married?"

Despite my question about Tom's job (as it turns out, he's a consultant of some kind), our Florida golf trip was like most great golf trips. Every day had the same agenda: wake up, drink coffee, eat bacon, play eighteen holes, eat cheeseburgers, play eighteen holes, drink beer, take shower, eat steaks, watch college basketball on TV, go to sleep. (My brother and I once went on a golf trip that was even better. Before playing our first eighteen holes each morning, we took a two-hour golf lesson; after eating dinner each evening, we watched a tape of that day's action at the Masters.)

The best golf trips, unlike vacations that wives plan, never leave you wondering what you are going to do next. There is never an empty three-hour time block in which you might suddenly be expected to look at churches, go shopping, read a book, or take a nap. You never have to wait between golf and beer, or between beer and shower, or between shower and dinner. When one agreeable activity ends, another begins.

There was only one day during our Florida trip that didn't proceed according to plan. It wasn't the day I asked Tom about his job. It was a day when we had finished our second round earlier than expected. There wasn't quite enough daylight left to play nine more holes, but there was still too much to eat dinner. What we ended up doing—I'm kind of ashamed to admit this—was tennis.

Perfecting Skins

TELEVISION TODAY PROVIDES such a wealth of golf-viewing opportunities that to complain about one of them seems impolite. But I'm complaining anyway: I don't like the Skins Game.

The main problem is that nothing important is at stake. The only real source of pressure for the participants (during a round of golf that, through the miracle of videotape, takes two days to play) is the possibility of being mildly humiliated by winning nothing. But that's not much of a narrative thread.

One way to enliven the Skins Game would be to require the competitors to play for something truly interesting, such as large piles of their own cash, lucrative endorsement deals, or spots on future Ryder Cup teams. But that's not likely to happen. If we want compelling skins matches, therefore, we're going to have to play them ourselves.

That's easy to do, luckily. I learned one excellent variant, called Escrow Skins, in Philadelphia a few years ago. Escrow Skins is just like regular skins—in which the object is to pile up cash by winning holes outright, with scores unequaled by other players—except that in Escrow Skins a player who wins money on one hole doesn't get to keep it unless he or she manages on the following hole to shoot no worse than some previously agreed upon score (such as net par or net bogey). Let's say that I make a brilliant birdie on the first hole while my three opponents stagger in with bogeys. I win a skin—worth a hundred thousand dollars in this example. But that skin doesn't go directly into my pocket; it sits in "escrow" while we play the second hole. If I screw up that hole with my usual post-birdie double-bogey, my skin goes back into the pot.

My Sunday morning group plays—as a supplement to our standard best-ball competition—a version of skins called Payball, which is easier than ordinary skins to manage with large groups. Before teeing off, every player throws five dollars into the Payball pot. At the end of the round, we compare scorecards and count up the number of skins that have been won across the entire group (with no carryovers). If there are eight skins, each is worth an eighth of the pot; if there are two, each is worth half.

The only problem with skins in any form is that players with low handicaps are usually at a disadvantage, since gross birdies and eagles are harder to come by than their net cousins. One corrective is to impose a handicap limit—or to eliminate strokes entirely on less demanding holes, such as par-threes and short par-fours. No matter what you do, though, you'll have more fun than you would sitting in front of the TV.

A year after I complained, in *Golf Digest*, about the TV Skins Game and described Escrow Skins as a more interesting alternative, the television show's producers adopted essentially the same format. Coincidence? Undoubtedly. (I would claim credit for the change, except that a majority of the show's viewers apparently didn't like the new format—although the players said they preferred it.) Since that time, though, I've discovered an even better skins game. My friend Tim invented it one autumn weekend not long ago, and my regular golf buddies and I have played it enthusiastically ever since. Tim's version eliminates all the weaknesses of the regular game. It's so good, in fact, that we call it Perfect Skins. Here's how it works:

Each player, on the first tee, throws in some mutually agreed-upon sum—say, ten bucks. That money is divided into two skins pools, one for the front nine and one for the back, and every skin won is worth a proportional share of its pool, as in Payball. (If three skins are won on the front nine, for example, each is worth a third of the front-nine skin pool; if a single player finishes with two of those three skins, he wins two-thirds of the pot.) The object is the same as in all skins games: to win holes outright, with scores unequaled by other players. But there's a twist: in Perfect Skins, a player who loses a hole outright, with a score that's worse than everyone else's, gives up a skin—or acquires a negative one, if he has none to give up.

Let's say the sixth hole is birdied by one player, parred by two players, and bogeyed by the fourth; in that case, the player with the birdie wins a skin while the player with the bogey loses one. (We call negative skins "Gillens," after the last name of the particular player whose long-running success at regular skins Tim was trying to thwart with his invention. Gillen hates Perfect Skins.)

Any player with a negative skin balance may buy himself back to zero before teeing off on any hole during the nine-hole match, at the price of one dollar* per negative skin, with the money going into the pool for that nine—but he may do so only once during the nine. That leads to the really interesting part of the game: Winning a skin when your balance is negative feels like a waste, because it merely moves you back toward zero rather than earning you a share of the pool. But buying back too early in a match raises the risk that one or two

---

*If you're one of those people who can't stand to play anything for a modest amount of money, you can obviously raise the stakes. You might want to use some multiple of these sums, though, because the proportions have been field-tested, and they work well. Speaking of high rollers: an obnoxious guest at a very famous golf club, the name of which you would recognize in an instant, once made a nuisance of himself by continually and loudly insisting on playing for bigger stakes than the members usually played for. Instead of a five-dollar nassau, he wanted to play a hundred-dollar nassau; instead of betting a penny a point in bridge, he wanted to play for a dollar. Finally, an annoyed member, who was almost incalculably rich, decided to shut him up. He said, "You seem to have quite a bit of money. Would you mind telling me your net worth?" The guest smugly said, "Twelve million dollars." The annoyed member snorted and said, "Aw, hell. I'll cut cards with you for that."

bad holes near the end of the nine could give you a deficit too large to eliminate before the end of the nine.

If you haven't used up your buyback yet, acquiring a negative skin is often less costly than permitting another player to win a positive one and thereby gain a share of the pool. That means that attempting a very risky shot may be to your advantage, if there's a chance that doing so will prevent another player from winning the hole, or if doing so will ensure an outright loss by a player who now has a positive balance—unless you yourself hold a couple of skins, in which case your best strategy may be to play defensively. A player who ends the nine with a negative skin balance—say, because he lost the final two holes outright—owes the pot two dollars for each negative skin still in his possession at the end of the nine.

Perfect Skins eliminates all the shortcomings of regular skins: it greatly reduces the influence of luck, because erratic players are punished for their disasters in addition to being rewarded for their fluky good fortune; it eliminates the high-handicap advantage, because the players with the most strokes are also the ones who are the most likely to suffer the kinds of disasters that lead to negative skins; it keeps everyone in the game, because not losing a hole can be just as important as winning it, and players who suffer a string of bad holes can redeem themselves by buying back into the game; it adds a new level of pressure, especially on the final tee, because skins aren't safe until the last putt has fallen.

Perfect Skins creates numerous opportunities for creative

skullduggery. In a recent match, for example, I hit a swell approach shot on the second hole, leaving myself a shortish but slippery sidehill putt for a birdie. Before I had to attempt it, John made a bogey, and Tim made a par. Then Ray faced a par putt of his own—which he intentionally missed, giving himself a bogey. Why? Because he knew that if he made a par, he would give me a free run at my birdie. He correctly assumed that I would putt less boldly if I knew I had to guard against three-putting, because a bogey from me would have handed the skin to Tim. (I made the putt anyway. Ha!)

I've played Perfect Skins in threesomes, foursomes, and fivesomes, and it works beautifully, though somewhat differently, in all those combinations. With three players, for example, the skin balance changes on every hole unless all three players tie—meaning that the standings can shift dramatically over just a few holes. With five players, in contrast, outright victories are harder to come by, so that a single skin successfully held to the end of the match could end up being worth the entire pool. In all combinations, the most important issue for any player with a negative balance is deciding when to buy back to zero. You have to think realistically about how well or poorly you're likely to play the holes that lie ahead, and who still has strokes, and where you yourself have strokes, and where you can afford to be aggressive.

My golf buddies and I are still happily working out the finer points of Perfect Skins; each time we play, it seems, we think of something new. Lately, we've been wrestling with the issue of whether players should be allowed to buy some sort of "skin insurance," to preserve one or more of the skins they've already won. We've already decided to allow conspiratorial side deals, in which a player agrees to miss a crucial putt in exchange for a share of another player's winnings.

We've also decided to allow private sales and purchases of skins. In a recent four-ball match, for example, I held two of the three skins outstanding by the time we got to the eighth hole, while Tony had none. After we teed off, Tony offered to buy one of my skins for five dollars, and I ended up selling it to him for six. That was slightly less than it would have been worth if I had held it to the end, but it assured me of coming out ahead on the nine no matter what I might do between that point and the end. Brother, this game goes deeper than chess.

Just Like the Pros

M Y RIGHT HAND FELT HEAVY when I woke up one morning, and my fingertips tingled. The tingling persisted through breakfast. I shook my hand, did a few pushups, and squeezed a rubber ball. The tingling persisted through lunch. I searched for my symptoms online and discovered that I was suffering—as I had suspected—from poor circulation, heart attack, stroke, diabetes, a herniated disk, a tumor, Guillain-Barré syndrome, or multiple sclerosis.

Pacing nervously through my house, I thought about how much I love my children, my wife, and our furniture. I fretted about whether to call my doctor. It was Saturday afternoon, and he was probably playing golf. Should I page him on the course or drive directly to the emergency room and schedule my own M.R.I.?

Thinking about golf and my doctor made me think about something else. With a flash of insight possibly comparable to Pasteur's realization that moldy bread can cure pneumonia, I was suddenly able to diagnose my malady as pseudo-carpal-tunnel syndrome brought on by sleeping in an awkward position while wearing one of those copper wristbands that Seve Ballesteros endorses. I removed the wristband—which was crimped against the underside of my arm like a staple in a stack of papers—and within an hour all my symptoms had disappeared.

Despite the side effects, I love my wristband. It supposedly cures arthritis—my dad wore one for that reason in the early seventies—but its main purpose is to declare that I am a serious golfer. Pretty many touring pros wear wristbands, as you'll discover if you study their arms on TV. Wearing one myself seemed like an easy way to become exactly like them.

When my wife first saw my wristband—which she called a bracelet—she laughed out loud, and I took it off for a while. But now I wear it all the time. It's a quarter-inch wide, and it leaves a stripe of green-blue residue around my wrist. I like the stripe almost as much as I like the wristband, which has begun to develop a deep, complicated patina, like that of fine old plumbing.

As for my arthritis, I'm undecided. Undecided, that is, about whether I have arthritis at all. I did break my right wrist in college, after being pushed off a ten-foot-tall fireplace mantel while dancing in a tuxedo. (When I came to, I was looking up into what in those days was quite a familiar sight for my friends and me: the scowling, downward-peering faces of campus policemen.) The doctor who operated on my arm told me that I might develop arthritis in middle age. My right wrist doesn't bend as much as my left wrist does, but that's been true since the cast came off. The reduced mobility worried me at the time, but the doctor was unconcerned. He asked me to bend both wrists as far as I could, then tapped the freshly healed one with his finger and said, "This is normal. The other one bends too much."

Local Knowledge

I SLIPPED AS I LOWERED MYSELF over an outcropping of rock, and I slid on my rear end for a good ten feet. But I picked myself up and kept going, because I was on an important mission. I was looking for something that had been missing for almost a hundred years. I was looking for a golf course.

Golf came to my town in 1893. It was brought by a physician from New York City, who built a summer house on the far side of the big hill on which my house stands. The doctor laid out a few crude holes on the slope behind his house, then invited his friends to join him in getting the hang of this fascinating new game, using equipment he had brought from New York. Golf was roughly half a millennium old, but it was just beginning to catch on in the United States. The first permanent golf club in America—the St. Andrews Golf Club, of Yonkers, New York—had only recently expanded from three holes to six, and the first United States Open was still two years away.

The doctor's summer house still exists, and is now owned by a friend of mine. It looks huge from the road but seems almost two-dimensional when viewed from either side, because it's just one room deep—a design innovation that was intended, in the era before air-conditioning, to promote cross-ventilation. Behind the house, at the edge of a steep ravine, is a simple wooden shed, which the doctor called his "golf house." My friend the current owner uses the shed to store old shutters and window screens, but the doctor created it for some golf-related purpose, now lost in time. If you stand on the only piece of level ground within a hundred feet of the shed and look down the hill, you can see what the doctor and his friends must have seen when, after balancing a lumpy ball on the peak of a small mound of wet sand, they took dead aim at the first green.

At least, I think you can. The doctor died a long time ago, as did everyone else who ever played his golf holes. I do know, though, that by the late 1890s the doctor's backyard and a neighboring sheep pasture had evolved into what in those days passed for a real golf club. There are a few photographs of parts of the course in the collection of our town's historical society, and another photograph hangs on the wall of a coffee shop on our village green. In almost all of the photographs, the principal subjects appear, to the untrained eye, to be sheep, which shared the ground and, serendipitously, maintained the turf. The course had nine holes, three of which were situated on the far side of a river and could be reached only by means of a crude floating bridge. A small covered shelter, made of stone and wood, stood beside one of the holes, and probably was used to protect golfers from sudden rainstorms; that shelter still stands, in the yard of another friend, and you can see it from the road. There were hardly any trees on the course, because almost all of them had been cut down, either to create grazing room for sheep or to make charcoal for iron-smelting, a major local industry in those days. The layout was tiny by modern standards. The whole thing probably didn't add up to much more than two thousand yards.

In the early 1900s, my town's first golf course was rendered obsolete by the introduction of the Haskell golf ball, which had a rubber core and flew much farther and straighter than the old gutta percha ball. (The Haskell had a bigger impact on the game than any subsequent technological innovation, including graphite shafts, jumbo drivers, and long-handled putters. Because of the Haskell, every golf course in the world had to be reconceived.) The doctor and his friends, now obsessed, laid out a new, longer nine-hole course, halfway across town, on forty acres of hilly pastureland and woods. That's the course where I play most of my golf today. Two of the fairways, the second and the eighth, are transected by anomalous rocky, grass-covered ridges, which are two or three feet wide and look a little like the fossilized vertebrae of gigantic dinosaurs, maybe; those are old stone walls, which were buried to take them out of play. Other walls, in the woods and around the edges of the course, are still standing. A narrow stream, which you can easily jump in dry weather, divides the entire property at its lowest elevation. The stream is dammed at one end, creating a small pond, which animates the nightmares of some of our shorter-hitting members, since it is very much in play from the fourth tee. (The right-hand end of the pond is known locally as Maine, and the left-hand end is known as Florida. The carry over Florida is twenty yards shorter than the carry over Maine.)

Each tee at the new golf club was equipped with a two-chambered concrete box about the size of a footlocker. One of the chambers in each box was filled with sand, and the other was filled with water. Before teeing off, a player would take a small amount of sand from the first chamber, dip his hand briefly into the second, and squeeze the damp lump into a tee. Wooden pegs replaced sand in the early nineteen hundreds, and the concrete boxes were discarded. When Bob, our superintendent, came to work here, in 1965, he found several of the old boxes half-buried in the woods. He rescued one of them and placed it, on its side, next to our first tee, where it remains today. Few current members are aware of its original purpose. It's a good place to set your coffee cup while you tee off.

Sometime in the early twentieth century, sheep-raising, charcoal-producing, and iron-smelting ceased to be the bulwarks of the local economy, and the original golf course was gradually obliterated by trees. One day not long ago, I decided to see if I couldn't find it, or parts of it. With my friend's permission, I climbed down into the ravine beside the doctor's old golf house, and tramped through the woods for a couple of hours. I walked along the riverbank and saw a field on the other side, where the three transriverine holes must have been, but I found no sign of the old floating bridge or its moorings. I noticed a couple of overgrown but relatively level areas in the woods which might have been tees or greens, although, in truth, they looked like nothing at all. I found grass growing among the trees in a few places where you wouldn't necessarily have thought grass would grow. (If the grass had, indeed, been a part of the golf course once, it had long since gone feral.) In all my looking, though, I found only one certain remnant of my town's original course: a boggy, weed-filled, stone-lined depression, which I recognized from a faded photograph as a former water hazard.

Sitting on the patio by our clubhouse later, I described my search to one of my club's old-timers; he drove home, and returned a short time later with an ancient gutta percha ball, which he gave to me. He said he had found it, years ago, wedged between two of the stones in the border of that same old water hazard. "You used to be able to find a lot of balls down there," he said, "but you probably can't anymore." The ball is smaller than a modern ball, and it has bumps instead of dimples, and it's as black as if it had been burned in a fire. I've never dared to take a full swing at it, but I did try chipping it once, on the carpet in my office. (It clacks rather than thumps when you hit it with a wedge.) I've got it on my desk right now. For some reason, I am pleased to think that, of all the shots ever struck on that vanished course, the only one to leave an enduring trace is one that landed in a pond.

Consistency

ON THE FIRST DAY of golf school several years ago, the instructors asked my fellow students and me what we hoped to learn. "Consistency," most of us replied. No matter how high our handicaps were, we all hit good shots from time to time—long drives, pure irons, steady putts. Our trouble, we figured, was that we hadn't learned how to hit those good shots all the time. All we wanted to know was how to repeat what we already knew.

Later, I realized that we had the problem backwards, or at least sideways. For most golfers, consistency is more nearly the disease than it is the cure. Our results may differ from shot to shot, but the flaws in our strokes are remarkably steady. I may hook from the first tee and slice from the second, but the swing that I use to hit both drives is as predictable as Nick Faldo's. My problem is not that I can't repeat. My problem is that I always do.

Muscle memory isn't something you have to work at, apparently. I have a friend who took up the game two years ago. He's had lots of lessons, and the lessons have helped him cut his handicap by a dozen strokes, but his swing today is nearly indistinguishable from the first swing he ever took. He has the same quick tempo, the same loopy dip, the same strange move with his left foot. I can pick him out from halfway across the golf course based on his practice swing alone, as I can most of the people I play with. Yet if you ask my friend what his game is missing, he'll say, "Consistency."

One of my classmates at golf school had a low, cramped swing in which he scarcely got his hands above the level of his elbows. The teachers moved his feet, changed his grip, and gave him drills to work on. "Oh, God, I can't believe how weird this feels!" he crowed at one point, thrilled to have had his game turned upside down. The rest of us glanced at one another in amazement: the guy looked exactly the same.

The explanation, of course, is that even a tiny change in a golf swing, like a speck of dust under your eyelid, can feel calamitously huge. When I take lessons, I'm like an addict in denial. My teacher coaxes me to make some minuscule adjustment in my take-away, while my agonized brain implores me to ignore him. "Go back to the rut you're used to," it whispers between swings. "This guy doesn't know what he's talking about. Are you sure he's even a pro?"

Most of our swing flaws are so deeply ingrained that getting rid of them would require, first of all, a monumental feat of unlearning. Never mind consistency. That's what got us into this mess in the first place. The thing we really need is amnesia.

Caddies

PEERING EAGERLY FROM AMONG the shadows in the farthest corner of the clubhouse porch were our new caddies. They were middle-schoolers, mostly. The older ones picked their teeth with tees and wanted to double-bag. The younger ones fussed with jackets their mothers had made them wear. They had arrived early, just as the old-timers were setting out with their squeaky pull carts. With luck, they would get to spend the rest of the morning earning twenty dollars and a free round on Monday.

Before a few years ago, there had been no caddies at my club for several decades. A man I sometimes play with remembers caddying here in the thirties. He earned thirty-five cents a round, sixty cents for two bags, and he once received a ten-dollar tip from Light Horse Harry Cooper, who was in town for the wedding of Horton Smith, the winner of the first and third Masters Tournaments. Another old-timer remembers caddying for Smith's father-in-law, Alfred Severin Bourne, who was one of the founders of Augusta National Golf Club. Bourne won our club championship in 1934, the year of the first Masters. He used to stand on our old practice tee and, with his five-iron, hit exactly thirty balls, which his caddie would scoop up in a leather bag. After counting the thirtieth shot, the caddie would run back to Bourne, who would play the first hole, chip to the eighth green, play the ninth hole, make the same circuit again, and go home. That home was a huge Tudor-style mansion, which looms over my house from the top of a hill, and serves today as the main building of a boarding school. (Bourne himself died long ago.)

One winter, our pro at the time, whose name was Zane, suggested that we try caddies again. Twenty kids turned up for training—a good showing in a town with a full-time population of two thousand. The credit belongs to Tiger Woods, who, among other feats, has managed to make golf attractive to sixth and seventh graders. Zane taught the kids where to stand, how to rake bunkers, when to speak, when to be quiet, and not to make suggestions.

Caddying is known to be morally uplifting for adolescents. They earn wages that are competitive with those paid to baby-sitters, learn to bounce golf balls on the faces of pitching wedges, and meet grownups who may one day give them some old irons or a job.

But the real beneficiaries are the golfers. Playing with young caddies allows adults to share the crises of juveniles without passing judgment, something that seldom happens at home. If your own child has a bad report card, you are likely to take it personally. If your caddie has a bad report card, you are likely to share a story about a bad report card of your own. A golfer who is willing to listen will hear a lot—about a broken bike, a teacher who's a jerk, a test on stuff that wasn't in the book, a father who's lost his job, a dog that almost died, a mother who is dating someone nice. The golfer responds as an adult rather than as a parent, and there is the same unspoken understanding that there always is among golfers: that what is discussed during the round will not leave the course.

One Saturday, there was a new caddie in our group. He was a fifth grader but looked two years younger. He carried Rick's bag, which was nearly as tall as he was, and on hills he had to lift it by the handle to keep it from dragging on the ground. Rain fell most of the morning, and by the time we finished his hair was pasted flat, his shirt was soaked, his sneakers were sloshing, and his legs were flocked with grass. Rick and I exchanged nervous glances over his head, anticipating the fury of his mother.

Next morning, I came out early to play again, and scanned the faces on the porch, expecting not to find his. But there he was, leaning over the railing to get a better look at the first tee, his jacket already abandoned. And he was smiling.

Winning

A FRIEND WHO KNOWS I'm interested in golf said, "I saw something at a garage sale that would have amused you. It was a box of old golf balls with Dean Martin on the—"

I cut him off. "You mean the 'Swinger's Dozen'? Thirteen balls, including 'one for the road'—with Dino's face on the box?"

My friend's jaw dropped. "How did you—"

"You snapped them up, I hope," I continued.

"No way," he said. "Guy wanted twenty bucks."

I groaned. A Swinger's Dozen in good condition usually goes for more than two hundred dollars on eBay, the Internet auction site. I bid on one but dropped out in the low three fig-ures. I felt depressed for a while, although I later recovered—probably because of all the other golf-related stuff I've bought (or "won," to use eBay's seductive term).

Here are some of my recent purchases: a golf-trophy-cum-desk-calendar with an emblem that says "National Amputee"; an old tin practice-ball bucket decorated with a color litho-graph of a guy at a driving range; a board game from the early sixties called Arnold Palmer's Inside Golf ("Learn Good Golf in the Living Room"); sheet music for a song called "Fore! Ike is on the Tee," copyright 1953; a box of Headown golf tees ("The Easy Way To Keep Your Head Down"), which are regular wooden tees attached to semi-realistic plastic representations of the lower halves of naked women; a porcelain planter in the shape of a ladies' golf shoe with a porcelain golf ball balanced on the toe.

All in all, I've probably spent two thousand dollars. That's a large sum, but it seems trivial when you realize how much I've saved by not bidding on tens of thousands of other items—such as a used plastic swizzle stick from the Green Jacket, a defunct restaurant in Augusta, Georgia, and a lot of seventy-two miscellaneous used golf balls, for which the seller wanted thirty-six dollars plus shipping. You might think that my wife, who hates golf, would be furious at me, but she's only mildly peeved, because she buys stuff on eBay, too. Recently, she picked up an autographed copy of *Mary Ann's Gilligan's Island Cookbook*, by Dawn Wells, who played Mary Ann. (Favorite recipe so far: Leaky Ship Watercress Soup.)

Our only problem now is storage. We have a nice big living room, but it's filled with stuff we didn't buy on eBay. To make room for our collection of golf-and-cooking memorabilia, we're going to have to deaccession some of our pre-Internet possessions, such as couches and chairs. That's fine with me but not with my wife, who's old-fashioned (so far) on the subject of furniture. If she ever changes her mind, though, I know where we can sell it all.

Father's Day

WE WERE STANDING AROUND drinking beer on Friday evening at my brother's member-guest a few years ago when one of the participants suddenly moaned, "Oh, [*very bad word*], I've got to go to my wife's [*extremely bad word*] birthday party." Nasty rub of the green, there. What are the odds of marrying someone who was born on the exact date of the steak-and-calcutta stag dinner? (My own wife's birthday occurs in the fall somewhere. No problem!)

At my brother's member-guest a couple of years later, I noticed that one of the regular participants was missing. "His wife wouldn't let him play," someone explained, "because it's Father's Day."

Let that one sink in for a moment.

I've always hated Father's Day without knowing why; now I know why: Father's Day has nothing to do with fathers. It's just a passive-aggressive reprise of the day that inspired it; it's Mother's Day, Part Two. You would think, in theory, that Father's Day would be the one Sunday of the year when a married man could get away with playing just as much golf and drinking just as much beer and smoking just as many cigars as he wanted to. But it doesn't work that way.

"Oh, you can't play golf in the morning," your wife says, smiling cruelly, "because the children have their hearts set on making you a nice Father's Day breakfast. And you can't play at lunchtime, because the children want to give you the presents they made for you at school. And you can't play in the afternoon, because your mother and I have planned a lovely Father's Day dinner for you and your dad." Which means, of course, that your father can't play, either.

Mother's Day, paradoxically, has a much higher Golfability Index than Father's Day does, because your wife isn't in charge of making the plans. You can buy her some jewelry, or you can make a dinner reservation for the two of you—say, at ten p.m., after the course has safely closed—or you can blow the whole thing off (she isn't *your* mother, after all) and endure her scorn for a week or two. If your kids are determined to serve her breakfast in bed, you can put a box of cereal on the kitchen counter before you leave for the club.

The only solution to the problem of Father's Day is to move it out of prime golf season. Will that require an act of Congress? I don't know, but here's what I propose: henceforth, Father's Day shall fall on the first rainy or snowy Monday in November. Like Passover, it shall begin at sundown. And it shall be ignored, or celebrated over the telephone, if you happen to be in Myrtle Beach with your pals.

Too Old for Golf?

In the late nineties, glimpses of Jack Nicklaus limping slightly—the result of arthritis in his hip—revived the old debate about whether he ought to hang up his clubs. "He should have quit after he won the '86 Masters," a friend of mine grumbled. That was the Masters, you will recall, when Nicklaus, who was forty-six, blind-sided a battalion of whippersnappers—among them Tom Kite, Greg Norman, Seve Ballesteros, and Nick Price—by finishing eagle-birdie-birdie-par.

Forty-six doesn't seem as old now as it did then. At least, it doesn't to me. Still, calling it quits from Butler Cabin would have been a breathtaking gesture, even in 1986. The model would have been the retirement of Bobby Jones, who gave up competition in 1930, after slamming the lid on the Grand Slam. Jones was twenty-eight and believed there were no worlds left to conquer. (He had also just negotiated a big golf-club-endorsement contract with Spalding and a huge instructional-film contract with Hollywood, and he wanted to keep the money but couldn't stand the thought of being known as a "professional.") Ever since then, great golfers who have played past their physical peaks have risked seeming like party guests who don't know when to go home. Sportswriters have even been known to cite A. E. Housman's "To An Athlete Dying Young"—*"Now you will not swell the rout / Of lads that wore their honor out"*—which can be read as advocating euthanasia for players with expired equipment deals.

People who side with Housman clearly believe that athletic achievements are frailer than eggs. They worry that if we watch Nicklaus missing greens and jabbing at putts, we'll forget what he was like when every tournament he entered was his to lose. Young fans—this line of thinking goes—won't be sufficiently impressed by the difference between him and Rives McBee. Why, they might even fail to realize that, back in the early sixties, Nicklaus was viewed as practically the next Tiger Woods.

This is exactly wrong, I think. Indeed, watching Nicklaus chop it around may be the only way ordinary mortals like you and me can even begin to get a handle on what he accomplished in his prime. Intact, his game was too good to comprehend. Like Tiger's, it was extra-human. Now that his swing has begun to falter, though, we can catch an occasional glimpse of how he must have put it together. We can see the seams that were invisible when he was twenty-five.

Bobby Jones had to be coaxed out of retirement to play in the first few Masters Tournaments, beginning in 1934. He didn't want to play, but he was persuaded that to refuse would be to doom the club, which was hanging by a thread financially and needed the tournament to attract the attention of potential members. As Jones had predicted, he was never a factor. But perhaps he was pleasantly surprised to discover that his fans didn't seem to mind, and that his gallery on the last day was larger than his gallery on the first. He had been embarrassed, initially, by the state of his short game, but by the time he finished on Sunday he was already looking forward to playing again the following year. And no one thinks less of him today for having been a good sport, even though by 1948, the last year he played, he could have used four or five strokes a side.

Besides, why should aging be hidden from the young? I don't intend to be packed off to a nursing home the first time I forget the dog's name—just as I didn't put my kids up for adoption when their cuteness crested, at the age of five. Getting older is a raw deal, but it's nothing to be ashamed of. Did *you* give up golf when you passed your prime?

The Greenkeeper's Tale

T HE COURSE RECORD at my club is 63, eight strokes under par. It was set in the early eighties by Bob Witkoski, our superintendent. His round is legendary among the few people who know about it, because it included three birdie putts that rolled to the rim of the cup but didn't fall. How those balls stayed out is an enduring mystery, because in that era our greens, which Bob himself maintained, were extraordinarily fast. A friend of mine who was a member then told me, "The grass on the greens didn't really even look like grass. It was just a sort of blue-gray haze." Bob's own conception of the ideal putting surface, he explained to me once, is "three inches of compacted dust." In the early eighties, Bob's greens were so firm that when players stood on them in metal spikes you could see sunlight between the ground and the soles of their shoes. "In those days," Bob says, "if you even looked at your ball it would start moving." The touring pro George Burns, who has relatives in our area, was a member of our club for a while. In 1982, he angrily walked in after playing four holes, and complained to Bob that the greens were unfairly fast. The year before, he had finished second in the United States Open, at Merion.

Many of the newer members of my club don't realize that Bob even knows how to play golf; they have never seen him swing a club. His record-setting round was one of the few serious rounds he has played in the past twenty years. Maintaining our golf course for almost four decades has ruined his back, and golf makes his back worse. He's also a perfectionist. He was an extraordinarily gifted player when he was in his teens, and I am fairly certain that he believed he had the potential not only to compete on tour but also, possibly, to be one of the best players ever. He worked on his swing late into the night in his room at home, doing permanent damage to the walls and the floor as he rehearsed his fundamentals. To develop strength in his arms, chest, and legs, he used to take golf swings with an axe.

The flip side of Bob's obsession was a feeling of fury that overcame him when he hit a shot that didn't meet his expectations. "Sometimes," he told me once, in a lowered voice, "I used to hit a bad shot on purpose." When he did that, I think, he was prodding the demon that haunted him, trying to bring it under his control. But control eluded him, and, in his heyday, a single bad swing could make him so angry he would give up the game for weeks. In a round with friends once, he got to six or seven under par after twelve holes, and had a six-foot putt for another birdie. His ball lipped the cup. He stood fuming silently for a moment, his eyes narrowed. Then he turned to the men he was playing with and said, "I don't think I owe you boys anything." He left his ball on the green, picked up his bag, and walked back to the parking lot. I've never dared to ask Bob what happened next, but I picture him sitting in the car alone for the next two hours, staring straight ahead and chewing his cigar. In the end, the only solution was to quit.

Bob did start playing again a little in the mid-nineties, because our pro at that time, whose name was Zane, was an old friend of his. Zane and Bob had played golf together years before, and Zane knew how to entice him into coming out for a few holes late in the afternoon. He also knew the kind of player that Bob had been in his prime. Bob is older than Zane, but they had played most of their golf at the same scrappy public course, in a town about a half-hour away from ours. (A friend who played there recently told me that all the tees had been equipped with boxes containing seed mix, for repairing divots, but that no one ever used them, apparently. The seed in the boxes had germinated, and big clumps of long, pale grass had pushed open the lids of the boxes and, like Rapunzel's hair, overflowed onto the ground.) The best regular players at that course were scrappy, too. They were blue-collar guys who had funny grips, odd swings, and weird putting strokes but somehow shot under par. I once played with two of them, old acquaintances of Bob's, in a local tournament, and they were so obnoxious that I almost quit after nine holes. They bragged and needled and complained and provoked, until I could scarcely swing. Bob was never like that. When he played, he was so quietly intense that he seemed almost fierce. But he loved beating those other guys, to whom he was (and still is) a legend.

"There was a big four-ball tournament at another club many years ago," Zane told me one day, "and I begged Bob to play in it with me. If I broke 80 in those days, that was a hell of a round for me, but we managed to qualify for the last spot in the championship flight, because of Bob. That meant we had to play the No. 1 team, and one of the guys on that team was the state amateur champion, and the other guy was one of the top local players. We went to the calcutta dinner after the qualifier, and the teams were going for five hundred, six hundred bucks, and the team that we were going to play went for the most, way over a thousand. Then they called our names, and there was complete silence. Before that, the room was buzzing, people were screaming and yelling and laughing— then, nothing. So Bob and I were kind of hunkered down at our table, embarrassed. Then the guy who was running the thing came over and gave us the bad news, which was that because nobody else wanted our team, we had to buy it ourselves, for fifty bucks. Which we didn't have. I said, 'We'll bring the money tomorrow,' and I ended up having to borrow it from the pro, who was a cousin of mine."

When Bob and Zane arrived on the first tee for their match the following morning, Bob was dressed as he often still dresses: in carpenter jeans—the kind with hammer loops—and a starched blue long-sleeved Oxford-cloth dress shirt. Zane was carrying an ancient set of flea-market clubs, including a putter with a hickory shaft. "The guys we were going to play weren't paying any attention to us," Zane told me. "They were standing over by the board, looking to see who they would have to play next, as soon as they got rid of us. I told Bob what they were doing, and he said, 'I'll show them who they have to play next.'"

The first hole was a three-hundred-and-twenty-yard par-four. Bob hit last. With his three-wood, he launched a huge drive far beyond the drives of the other players, and his ball rolled up near the fringe of the green. He chipped it close and sank the putt, for birdie. The second hole was a long par-four, a dogleg to the right. The standard strategy for playing the hole was to hit a driver straight down the fairway, past the corner, leaving about a five-iron to the green. That's what Zane did. Then Bob teed up his ball and aimed to the right, directly toward the trees that flanked the fairway. The trees were tall and thick, but Bob carried them all with his three-wood, and his ball ended up in the middle of the fairway, just a wedge from the green.

"He stiffed it and made the putt," Zane said. "We had played two holes, and Bob was two under on his own ball, and we were two-up in the match. And for the guys we were playing, it was downhill from there. I only helped on one hole. Bob drove it through the fairway on a dogleg, and I had to make a par. Bob said, 'Make this putt, and they'll be done.' I made it, and that's what happened. They couldn't believe it.

The No. 1 team, and all of a sudden they weren't in the tournament anymore."

During the two years when Zane was our pro, he occasionally was able to talk Bob into playing with him in one of the Monday pro-ams that our state golf association conducts. Bob, inevitably muttering, would retrieve his clubs from his garage and throw them into the trunk of Zane's car. Bob's bag is made of some early, abandoned version of vinyl, and his irons are a kind you never see anymore: Spalding Top-Flite Professionals, which he bought in 1965. The blade of his two-iron is the size and thickness of a jumbo paperclip. My friend Rich says he once watched Bob use that two-iron to hit the greatest golf shot he has ever personally witnessed: a two-hundred-yard hole-in-one in driving wind and rain on the next-to-last hole of a local four-ball tournament. Bob's shot squared the match. According to Rich, you could tell the ball was in the hole the moment it left the club.

All of Bob's clubs have faces that are pitted with rust. They also have leather grips, which look as though they were cut from the straps of old cavalry saddles. Upon arriving with Zane at one Monday pro-am a few years ago, Bob handed his bag to an attendant, gave him a couple of bucks, and said, "Just wipe the mildew off of these, if you wouldn't mind." He wasn't being funny; the grips really were covered with mildew.

At that same tournament, Bob and Zane were grouped with a terrific young player, who is the head pro at a Donald Ross course in our area. Bob played comfortably for a while;

in fact, he birdied five of the first eight holes. Then a stabbing pain in his back began to play havoc with his swing, and between shots he had to brace his spine against the seat of his golf cart. The young pro ended up shooting 64, which was one stroke short of the tournament record. Quite a round— although he and Bob had a side match going, and when Bob's back gave out, at the turn, the young pro was one-down.

Bob is about sixty years old, and he has a bristly mustache that has gone mostly gray. I could probably count on two hands the number of times I have seen him, during the past decade, when he wasn't smoking a skinny, irregularly shaped cigar. Except for his back, he's in terrific shape. He usually wears a golf hat, a pair of lightly-tinted aviator sunglasses with plastic rims, and a nylon windbreaker in which embers from his cigars have melted a constellation of small holes. The legs of his pants end above the tops of his shoes, a fashion preference dictated by the hours he spends ankle-deep in wet grass. When he hand-waters a green or a patch of burned-up turf, he doesn't use a spray nozzle on his hose, because he doesn't like what spray nozzles do to the flow of water. Instead, he shapes the stream with his thumb, the end of which, by now, is virtu- ally nerveless and slightly beveled. As he works, he usually keeps his back turned to any golfers who happen to be nearby. Years of handling loud machinery have made him hard of hearing, a condition he supplements with a form of selective deafness that makes it difficult for him to hear anything he doesn't want to hear.

A few years ago, Bob suffered an attack of kidney stones, a recurrent ailment of his. Diane, his wife, was out of town, and Bob stubbornly writhed on the floor of his living room all alone for several hours. Finally, no longer able to tolerate the agony, he crawled to the telephone and called Ferris, who is a former chairman of our golf club. Ferris is the only member of the medical profession who has ever won Bob's trust. When Bob's back is really killing him, he will sometimes drive over to Ferris's office and ask him to take a look. Ferris is a veterinarian. Among the records in the files at his animal hospital is a chart on which the name of the patient is listed as "Bob" and the name of the patient's owner is listed as "Diane Witkoski." (On the night of the kidney-stone attack, Ferris took Bob to the emergency room of a hospital for people.)

My club hired Bob to be its superintendent in 1965. He was just out of high school, and he had acquired the sum total of his golf-course-maintenance experience the summer before, when he worked as an assistant to the superintendent of another nine-hole course in our area. My club sent him to agronomy school at a big university in a neighboring state. When Bob returned, he faced an impossible task. Our course covered just forty acres, or a little more than half of the United States Golf Association's recommended minimum for nine holes. The property was rolling, open pastureland transected in a few places by old stone walls and narrow streams. There were wooded areas beyond the perimeter and alongside one of the streams, but the course itself was mostly just a large empty field. On the one big dogleg, a par-five, the members were essentially on their honor to stay within the lines. If you had removed the flags from the greens, the property from a distance would have looked very much the way it looked in the nineteenth century, when a local farmer kept sheep there. You wouldn't even have noticed a difference between fairway and rough, because the club's rusting gang mower cut all the grass to the same height.

One of the first things Bob did was to plant more trees. He planted hundreds of them—white pines, blue spruces, oaks, maples, willows, birches, cherry trees, apple trees, pear trees, and others, and he planted rhododendrons, mountain laurels, and other flowering shrubs. (The club had no capital-improvement budget in those days; the trees were paid for by a couple of wealthy members.) Bob didn't just stick the trees anywhere; he used them to define the course, and to create a strategic logic for the holes. Sometimes after playing one of those holes for a while, he would change his mind and move a few trees around. Today, all the trees Bob planted are mature. They seem so much like a part of the course that I almost can't believe there was ever a time when they weren't there, even though I've seen old pictures.

Bob's extensive plantings also, in time, made our course a compatible habitat for a diverse assortment of wildlife. If you yank a three-wood into the oaks along the left side of the sixth fairway, half a dozen flashes of blue and orange will sometimes burst from the canopy: bluebirds. One year, a ruffed grouse took a liking to Bob and would emerge from the woods near the ninth green whenever he walked past; once, it followed his daughter into their house. Bob fed it cracked corn from a jar, which he kept under a blue spruce beside the back tee on six. (Sometimes, one member of a foursome playing from that tee would have to distract the bird while the other three teed off.) At various times, I have spotted screech owls, snapping turtle hatchlings, red-tailed hawks (one of which often hangs out in a maple that Bob planted beside the seventh green), ring-necked pheasants, red foxes, jack rabbits, deer, a day-old fawn (which was curled up in the scrub to the right of the sixth fairway), mink, raccoons, possums, beavers, woodchucks, skunks, great blue herons, and a pileated woodpecker. One summer, my friend Tim and I saw a bald eagle snatch a fish from the pond on four and fly in low circles above the fourth fairway with its meal gripped in its talons. The year before, I watched from the practice tee as a bobcat nonchalantly circled a flock of wild turkeys, which were loitering nervously in the middle of the driving range.

Bob loves the wildlife on our course, but he is not a sentimentalist. He has built several hunting stands in the woods outside the perimeter, and he shoots a deer almost every winter. He also ice-fishes on the pond. In addition, he is merciless toward any creature that threatens the turf. One summer, a friend of mine was talking with him near the upper tee on the third hole. Bob froze in mid-sentence, got out of his cart, and began to creep slowly down the steep, brush-covered hill that separates the upper tee from the middle one. At the bottom, he stood motionless for a moment, then leapt forward, jammed his heel into the ground, thrust a screwdriver into the turf, and flipped out a mole, which for several days had methodically been ruining the tee. "Got the bastard," Bob said. He kicked the corpse into the weeds, wiped the blade of his screwdriver in the grass, and went back up the hill to finish his conversation with my friend. (Late one afternoon, I ran into Bob and Diane, who were taking a walk on the course. Bob was carrying a wide-mouthed iced-tea bottle, in which he had imprisoned a live star-nosed mole. In deference to his wife, Bob had somehow managed to capture the mole rather than skewering it at the end of its tunnel.)

Quite understandably, Bob is especially protective of our greens, and he takes their health personally. (He and Diane were married, in 1974, in front of the fourth green, which he had just expanded. Many members attended the ceremony. It was conducted by the club's president, who happened to be a justice of the peace.) Bob seldom had access to heavy equipment when he first began; his principal green-shaping tools in those days were a shovel, a rake, and the trunk of his Rambler sedan, which he used to haul topsoil. Once he had the contours the way he wanted them, he used his boots to tamp down the soil until it was "foot-tight," he told me once. Several of our greens are steeply sloped from back to front, but there is no trickery in any of them: You can see the break; do you have the nerve to putt it? Bob always did. "Even in the days when greens were like Formica," he once said, "I always wanted to be above the hole." He is a frighteningly good putter still, when he plays. One Sunday morning a couple of years ago, he played along with my regular group, using only a sixty-year-old adjustable club, which he had set to the loft of a six-iron. He used that club for every shot, including putts. If we hadn't ungraciously disqualified him after the fact, he would have won two skins.

One of Bob's biggest projects involved our third green, which had to be moved thirty yards to the left because it continually came under bombardment from slicers teeing off on the second hole. I once asked him if he had transplanted the sod from the old green to the new one, and he told me he hadn't. He had no use for the old turf, he said, so he brought down his seven-iron and a large supply of practice balls, and methodically flayed the original putting surface to the exact depth of his swing, hitting sweet shot after sweet shot, and littering the fairway below it with perfectly rectangular divots. He told me that destroying that green with his seven-iron was the most fun he ever had hitting practice balls.

When Bob had to expand or rework one of our greens, he didn't follow the U.S.G.A.'s specification for putting-green construction—a sort of standard blueprint that is used by golf-course builders all over the world—because he felt it was misguided. (One of his complaints was that the original specification called for what he believed was too much sand. He felt gratified, years later, when the U.S.G.A. apparently reached a similar conclusion.) Bob also disapproves of almost all modern turf strains. As a result, some of our greens are living museums of heirloom grass varieties, each of which Bob has patiently nursed along for decades, and none of which are commercially available today.

Several years ago, when Bob was doubling the size of our practice green, he showed me what he doesn't like about modern grasses. "The blades are too fat," he said, pulling a tiny clump from the new section, and holding it up next to a similar clump from the old. I could easily see the difference. The new grass was greener, plumper, and more robust-looking, despite the fact that it was theoretically the same species and had been maintained identically.

"Why is that bad?" I asked.

"You can't make the new grass roll as fast and true as the old, because the blades are so thick they affect the ball," he said. In the early eighties, when our greens were at their best, Bob starved the grass to pale wisps, like the nap on a piece of felt. Modern turf is too hearty for that. (Our course now gets too much play to support pale, wispy greens, unfortunately.

Our greens today are nowhere near as fast as they were twenty years ago, although they are still almost as true.)

Because Bob is adamant about protecting our putting surfaces, our club is almost always the first one in our region to close for the winter and the last to open in the spring, making our playing season at least a month shorter than the playing seasons of other clubs nearby. A few years ago, a number of us began to wonder whether Bob's exactitude wasn't mainly just a product of his orneriness, and whether there wasn't something we could do to extract more golf from our course. Our long-range planning committee, of which I was a member, hired an agronomist from the green section of the U.S.G.A. to inspect our turf. What we wanted the agronomist to tell us was that there was no reason to close so early and open so late. When Bob found out what we were up to, he was deeply, though quietly, affronted.

At the beginning of the inspection, the U.S.G.A. agronomist, who was quite young, gave a brief introductory speech, during which Bob took many shallow puffs on his cigar. Then the agronomist turned to Bob and asked, "How often do you aerify your greens?" Aerification is a standard golf-course maintenance procedure. A machine that looks a little like an enormous lawn mower is used to punch thousands of holes in each putting surface. The holes permit air to circulate among the roots of the grass, and they help to eliminate thatch, which is a spongy accumulation of dead material that blocks air flow and promotes disease. Many superintendents aerify their greens twice a year.

"I aerified five of the greens thirteen years ago," Bob said through clenched teeth, "and I haven't done any of them since."

The agronomist looked horrified. Under further questioning, Bob explained that he didn't like to poke holes in turf unless doing so was absolutely necessary, because he felt that such holes merely provided entry points for diseases, weeds, and undesirable varieties of grass. Looking doubtful, the agronomist picked up an implement that resembled a pogo stick with a metal scoop attached to one end. He walked over to the old part of the practice green, near which we had been sitting, and plunged the scoop into the putting surface. He pulled it back out, flipped open a metal gate on the side of the scoop, and revealed a soil sample that was roughly the size and shape of a slice of wedding cake. The earth in the sample was as black as espresso grounds. Dangling from the bottom, like the tentacles of a jellyfish, was a mass of filamentous roots.

The agronomist was silent for a moment, then said, "That's just about the healthiest-looking sample I've ever seen."

In his written report, which he mailed to us later, he said that although regular aerification of greens is a universally recommended procedure, Bob's "other cultural practices" apparently "make this aerification unnecessary." He also backed up Bob's restrictions on the use of our greens in the

early spring and late fall. "The inconvenience caused by the
delayed opening," he explained, "is minimal in comparison to
the benefits which are obtained with the improved turf conditions and surface quality through the entire summer season."
After that, we never mentioned experts to Bob again.

Half a dozen years ago, I watched the final match of our club
championship from the passenger seat of a golf cart, which I
was sharing with our pro at the time, Zane. On the eighth tee,
a young kid named Galen—who had beaten me easily in the
semifinal the day before, and would go on to win the title by a
wide margin—hit a huge drive far down the center of the fairway. One week before, Galen had shot 69 in the qualifying
round, while the next best score was something like 78. He
was one of the longest hitters our club had ever had. His tee
shot on eight that day sailed over a weed-covered mound that
most of our members never worry about reaching. His ball
ended up perhaps fifty yards short of the green, and I turned
to Zane and asked, "How the hell does he hit the ball that far?
His swing looks so easy."

"Don't you recognize that swing?" Zane said. "That's
Bob's swing."

Galen has a loop at the top of his backswing that Bob
doesn't approve of, but his power, simplicity, and apparent
ease are, indeed, highly Boblike. And for good reason: Bob

taught Galen to play. Galen's father, Brendan, is a contempo-
rary and a golf buddy of mine. He works as a lineman for the
local power company, and he counts the days until he can
retire. Brendan caddied at our club in the early sixties, when
he was a young boy. In his era, veteran caddies hazed novices
by forcing them to run from the clubhouse to the stop sign at
the end of Golf Course Road and back in just their underpants. Caddying got Brendan interested in golf, and Brendan's
interest eventually captivated Galen, who started playing at
the age of eleven or twelve. Bob noticed him and took a pro-
prietary interest in his swing.

Bob's conception of the golf swing is tantalizingly simple.
"There's nothing complicated about it," he likes to say. "You
just take the club straight back and then swing it straight
through." This motion seems a lot simpler when Bob
describes it or performs it than when you yourself try to repli-
cate it, but something about Bob's ideas clicked with Galen. In
those days, my club didn't have a real driving range (because
Bob hadn't built one for us yet). Galen would go over to the
course late in the afternoon and hit balls on the far side of the
sixth fairway while Bob looked on. When Galen played, Bob
would often observe him from a distance—while mowing an
adjacent fairway, say. If Bob noticed something that needed
attention, he would call Galen over and tell him what he
thought he ought to do.

Galen was the medalist in the first high-school tournament
he played in, as a freshman, and he continued to improve from

there. He won match after match, and played in college, and won our club championship two years in a row. Half a dozen pretty good middle-aged players at my club were quietly relieved when he finally graduated from college and got a job in San Francisco.

One day several years ago, when Galen was visiting from college, he and his father and my friend Ray and I played a round together. We ran into Bob on our club's fourth hole, a par-five. We were playing that hole from the farthest tee, which Bob built back in the early eighties for the touring pros Ken Green and Mark Calcavecchia, who, like George Burns, had family in our area and used to play at our club sometimes. (Green was a member briefly; Calcavecchia would sometimes jump on the gang mower and cut the rough when Bob was short-handed, as he usually was. Bob says it was he who persuaded Calcavecchia to abandon his hook and adopt a fade— one of the keys to Calcavecchia's success as a pro, Bob believes.) Bob was pruning some trees near the tee. He watched us hit our drives, then talked with us for a while.

"Hit one," Galen said.

"Nah," Bob said. "I haven't swung a club all year."

"Come on. Just one."

Galen set a ball on a tee. I held out my driver. Bob looked at the club. Finally, he put down his loppers.

He didn't take a practice swing. He didn't make a waggle. He glanced once at the fairway. "This could go anywhere," he said. Then he drew the club straight back, until the ash at the end of his cigar just brushed the shoulder of his jacket, and he swung. His ball took off high and straight, toward the only part of the fairway from which you can reach the green with a middle iron. The ball stopped where it landed, on the center mowing stripe, fifteen yards past Galen's ball.

"Missed it," Bob said, and he handed back my driver. It was a pretty long time before any of us could think of anything to say.

Too Many Clubs?

U NLESS THE UNITED STATES GOLF ASSOCIATION raises its club limit from fourteen to two hundred and twelve, I am someday going to have to face the fact that I have wasted some very serious money on golf equipment. I don't regret any of my purchases individually, but I am disquieted when I consider them in the aggregate. My collection of clubs, even if viewed solely as scrap metal, represents a major investment. A cupboard in my basement contains nothing but superfluous head covers.

In truth, though, even fourteen clubs is probably too many. One weekend, my Sunday-morning group imposed a five-club limit on the day's competition, as a novelty. I chose my putter, sand wedge, eight-iron, six-iron, and three-wood—a fairly typical line-up, it turned out. Surprisingly, I shot about what I usually shoot, and so did everyone else. In fact, the score of the winning foursome that morning was two shots better than the score of the winning foursome the week before, when we had observed no limit on hand luggage more stringent than the U.S.G.A.'s.

The day's results lent a meditative air to the beer-swilling after the round. "Maybe we ought to play with five clubs all the time," someone said—and the comment, unlike most post-round comments, was received with thoughtful reflection. Someone else pointed out that the scores during our club's annual two-club tournament, which had been held a few weeks before, had been indistinguishable from regular scores—except for the score of one guy, who had managed to post a new personal best. "Maybe I should get rid of everything except my pitching wedge," a third player said. And so forth.

Before the end of the week, naturally, we had all gone back to drooling over Golf Channel infomercials, and I myself became powerfully attracted to a set of irons that I spotted in a mail-order catalogue. But I still brood about how well I played that Sunday with just a fraction of my legal allotment.

Maybe the number of clubs we carry is less important than the selection. Five clubs may truly be all I need—as long as none of the five is a driver, a long iron, or the elusive Unhittable Club of the Day (U.C.D.), which moves unpredictably around my golf bag. One day, for no clear reason, my U.C.D. was my seven-iron; the next, it was my five-wood. The five-wood meltdown was especially unsettling, because that club is the one I turn to when nothing else is working off the tee. In a panic, I took it out of my bag, threw it in the trunk of my car, and promptly forgot all about it. When I finally thought of it again, a couple of weeks later, it had somehow resolved its disagreement with my swing, and had gone back to working fine.

The Beer Draw Hypothesis

W HILE COMPETING in an amateur tournament in Florida several years ago, my friend Rich and I developed a theory of the golf swing whose central proposition is that the difference between a slice and a draw is a certain number of beers. Our discovery arose from the scientific fact that tension in the arms usually ruins a golf swing, by promoting a slice. Since sobriety is a leading cause of tension, mightn't beer offer a solution? A moderate infusion of alcohol, we surmised, ought to have the same relaxing effect on the arm muscles of banana-prone golfers that it is said to have on the inhibitions of attractive strangers in bars. In fact, this effect has long been suspected by golfers, who refer to alcoholic beverages as "swing oil"—making this yet another instance in which a modern medical breakthrough was anticipated by an ancient folk remedy.

Over the course of many rounds in Florida, Rich and I set out to determine the exact level of intoxication required to cause our tee shots to move consistently from right to left. As is well known, excessive consumption of alcohol can be every bit as bad for golf as clenched biceps are. A golfer who is too loose tends to hit big hooks, big slices, and impotent sky balls, and he may also fall over while lining up putts. That's one reason why corporate golf outings have such a bad reputation. Furthermore, golfers who have eliminated too much tension from their swing will sometimes drive their cart onto a green. How can a golfer secure the maximum advantages of the beer draw without making it hard for everyone else to putt?

After careful study and much learned debate, Rich and I concluded that the ideal swing-oil dosage is one and a half beers, or the equivalent, administered fifteen minutes before teeing off and then carefully maintained throughout the round. Not surprisingly, the maintenance poses the main difficulty. A golfer who has drunk one and a half beers before playing is seldom willing to wait until reaching, say, the third hole before taking another swig. Ideally, therefore, the beer should be administered steadily and intravenously, under the supervision of a registered nurse, who might also serve as a caddie. (In the real world, sadly, the average golfer is usually forced to depend on his own sense of restraint, which the very treatment has a well-known tendency to impair.)

Relying on beer to encourage an inside-to-outside swing path may seem quaint, given recent advances in psychopharmacology. I asked Rich, a pharmacist, whether he thought Prozac would make us both better putters. He said he didn't know; the research hadn't been done. But it seems obvious to me that antidepressant drugs must offer hope. Anxiety and obsessive fear of failure are among the principal enemies of a smooth putting stroke, and Prozac alleviates both conditions. Curiously, though, my own physician later declined to write me a prescription, saying that a tendency to jab at the ball under pressure was not among published indications of any known medication.

Of course, alcohol and antidepressants are mere palliatives. The real problem is that human evolution has followed a course that is inimical to golf. Neurologically speaking, the human brain is way too big. All those folds and creases and networks of neurons are a hopelessly fertile breeding ground for golfing disasters. The ideal brain for golf would be mostly spinal cord—probably about the size of a clenched fist. There would be enough synapses to enable you to move your putter back on line, but not so many as to leave you torn between a hard six and a smooth five. An added bonus: Play would move faster, because there would be no distracting conversation.

Caddying for Friends

TEN YEARS AGO, my friend Art caddied for my friend Jim in the chump flight of our club championship. When Art showed up on the practice tee with a damp towel draped over his shoulder, Jim's opponent threw a fit. "You can't have a caddie," he said. "It isn't fair." Art's handicap was very low, and Jim's and his opponent's were very high. With Art reading Jim's putts, the opponent complained, Jim would have an unreasonable advantage.

Our pro overruled his objection, naturally, and, using the rule book, proved to him that caddies are as much a part of golf as bunkers and casual water. Jim's opponent remained upset, however. Conciliatorily, Art agreed to turn around whenever he swung, so as not to make him nervous. (Jim kicked his butt.)

Since that time, members caddying for members during important tournaments has gradually become a tradition at my club. Friends caddie for friends, fathers for sons, brothers for brothers, victims for victors. When the results of the club-championship qualifier are posted, players who've missed the cut often offer to loop for those who've made it. Caddying takes some of the sting out of the octuple-bogey that kept you from advancing to match play. It also turns an individual match into a team event, and, in a thought-provoking way, inverts the chemistry of rivalry.

I've caddied for several friends over the years, and several friends have caddied for me; mostly, I've caddied for my friend Ray, who is one of my club's best players. One year, when he and I met in the first round of a big tournament, we agreed that the loser of our match would caddie for the winner the rest of the way. That was pretty much the same thing as my agreeing that I would caddie for him, since he was the defending champion and I had barely survived the qualifier. And, in fact, that's the way it worked out.

Caddying is a challenge because it requires you to maintain a precise but shifting balance between involvement and invisibility. My worst failure as a caddie came during the final round of the club championship one year, when, intoxicated by the emotion of the match, I loudly disputed a rules interpretation made by our pro. My biggest contribution occurred during the same tournament a few years before, on a par-five where Ray had hit his drive into a terrible position from which to go for the green. Ray is a stubborn, aggressive player, and he doesn't like to lay up. He took a long look at his lie, though, and said, morosely, "I guess I should just knock it down there with a wedge"—the sensible play, and, as he knew, exactly what I myself would have done.

But I swallowed hard and said, "That doesn't sound like you." The gloomy look vanished from his face. With palpable relief, he took his three-wood, and—from a sidehill, downhill lie—hammered his ball just short of the green. It was a reckless shot, which I would never have attempted and could never have pulled off. But (as I had to keep reminding myself that day) I wasn't the guy playing the match.

Every fall, ten players from my club play a two-day match against ten players from a rival club. The other club's team always looks superior on paper, but, during the past decade, the team that has won the trophy most often has been ours. One of our advantages, I've begun to think, is the complicated bond we've built in our big tournaments. Caddying for one another has made us allies as well as rivals. In events in which we play together as a team, we know how to help one another win.

A Little Help
from a Friend

THE GREAT BRITISH GOLF CORRESPONDENT Henry Longhurst once recounted (with disapproval) an old joke about a golfer who was "alternately playing and kicking his ball" because he was "practicing for the mixed foursomes." Longhurst loved foursomes—in which two golfers take turns playing the same ball, a game that in this country is better known as "Scotch foursomes" or "alternate shot"—and he especially loved mixed foursomes, in which each team consists of a man and a woman. I don't know many golfers who would agree. But I do understand what he meant.

The first time I played nine holes in thirty-six strokes, I did it in a spring mixed-foursome event, as the partner of the wife of a friend of mine. We didn't look like a promising team. Her handicap was forty-five or fifty, and we had never played together before, and my swing hadn't fully thawed from a long, snowy winter. We teed off with no expectation of doing well. After three or four holes, though, I realized that we had made only pars. When my partner hit a bad shot, I somehow followed it with a great one, and when I left a twenty-foot putt five feet short, she somehow stuffed it in the hole. We double-bogeyed the sixth, a par-four, despite having been twelve feet from the cup in two, but we closed with a chip-in birdie on the ninth. We won both gross and net by a shocking number of shots.

How had we managed to play so much better as a team than either of us was then capable of playing alone? The answer, I think, is that foursomes can fool you into playing golf the way great competitors do instinctively. When you stand over a bunker shot in a foursome match, your arms don't tense up with embarrassment and regret, because it wasn't your slice that put you in the sand. And when you line up a six-foot putt, you don't panic, because you know the come-backer, if there is one, won't be your responsibility. In foursomes, you can only be a hero. The problems you are asked to solve are not problems that you yourself created, and if you make a mess, someone else has to clean it up. You focus only on the task at hand—just as the great golf teachers say you should.

(Unfortunately, none of this applies to married couples, who bicker like tennis players. Best advice: play with a stranger.)

"Do You Golf?"

Ordinarily I'm not a language snob. Does it really matter if people incorrectly refer to concrete as "cement," or say "fortuitous" when what they really mean is "serendipitous," or use "enormity" as a synonym for "immensity," or complain about their "arteriosclerosis" when what they actually have is atherosclerosis (unless it's the other way around)? Life is too short for brooding about the vocabularies of strangers.

And yet.

Surely you, too, have noticed that half the people in America now unashamedly use *golf* as a verb: *Do you golf? My brother-in-law golfs. Have you ever seen Tiger Woods golf? My wife and I golfed on our honeymoon. I'm thinking of teaching my cat to golf.* People who speak this way are almost always non-players or neophytes. It's your great-aunt, not David Duval, who asks you if you "golfed" over the weekend. The pro at your club doesn't "golf." The other members of your foursome don't "golf." And Ben Hogan never "golfed" in his life.

This linguistic form is unique to our game, incidentally.

Nobody tennises, or baseballs, or billiardses, or soccers. The people who use *golf* as a verb could cite the dictionary in their defense, but the dictionary is not enough: the word just doesn't sound serious. Using *golf* as a verb is like using *sex* as a verb (a usage permissible only for people who hold very unglamorous jobs in the poultry industry). Using *golf* as a verb demeans our noble game.

I don't mind *golfer* (although a few purists insist on *player*). I can even stand an occasional *golfing*. But the entire conjugation of *to golf* makes me want to grab a four-iron and golf somebody in the head with it.

While we're on the subject of golf-related annoyances, let's spend a moment on ball washers. Beginning players are always easy to spot: They store their tees in wrist bandoliers, they keep score with a mechanical clicker, and they can't pass a ball washer without using it. You hear them pumping as you tee up your first drive of the morning; you hear them pumping as you consider your final putt of the afternoon. These new golfers need to be told that ball washers serve a decorative function only, and are never to be used. Real golfers clean their balls by spitting on them and rubbing them on their thighs, making a stain that dry-cleaning can't remove, and identifying them as players, not as people who golf.

Going Spikeless

THERE WAS MUCH GRUMBLING at my club a few years ago, when we were debating whether or not to ban metal spikes. Members complained that they would lose yardage, flub shots from the rough, slide on the tee, stumble on the clubhouse steps, and break their necks climbing in and out of bunkers. But there was almost no grumbling after the new rule went into effect. Our plastic nubs grip the ground as firmly as the eight-penny nails we used to wear. Our greens are healthier, walking is easier, and you can stop by the grocery store on your way home from the course without taking off your golf shoes. The slip-and-fall lawyers who were going to kill the club with lawsuits have gone back to their hundred-dollar nassaus.

Our spikeless policy has not been without negative consequences, however. Putts roll better, yes, but something subtle has changed: Golf at my club, and at clubs all over America, doesn't sound the same anymore. The old hail-on-a-tin-roof clatter of foursomes loitering outside the pro shop has disappeared. Like the songs of cicadas, it was a sound that became louder when it stopped. The golfers now come and go on little cat feet, like Carl Sandburg's fog.

It's hard to trace an obsession to its source, but there must be more than a few golfers today who were first attracted to the game by the sound of steel on pavement, the summer sound of fathers. Junior golfers used to yearn for the day when their feet would stop growing, so they could graduate from sneakers. Now, we all sound like tennis players. The only solution I can imagine would be to equip the soles of golf shoes with electronic gizmos that would clack when you stepped on something hard. The technology exists. My son used to have a pair of sneakers that flashed as he walked.

The problem is that the main function of metal spikes is not to grip the ground but to declare golf a sport and not a game. Spikeless, a golfer could pass for a bowler. The cautious, abbreviated stride of a golfer in metal spikes walking from the pro shop to the first tee was indistinguishable from the cautious, abbreviated stride of a football player in steel-tipped cleats descending from the locker room to the playing field. Spikes made golf sensuously destructive. The gnawed porches at Myopia, the worn brick terraces at Pinehurst, the dimpled rear bumpers of rental cars on the Monterey Peninsula: a man likes to leave a little damage in his wake.

For all the poignant associations, though, metal spikes will not return. Once golfers have had a taste of tuftless greens, they lose their yearning to go back. At my club one day, a member on his way to becoming an ex-member made one of his thankfully rare appearances at the golf course and refused to have his shoes neutered. He yelled at the pro, pushed his way past the assistant pro, and played anyway. If he expected sympathy from the rest of us, he was mistaken. All afternoon, golfers kept coming to the pro shop and complaining: "Hey, there's somebody out there in *spikes*."

Dressing for Golf

Not long ago, in a national daily newspaper, a veteran sportswriter referred to the PGA Tour as "the polyester pack." I got the joke—but isn't that gag at least fifteen years out of date? Golf's era of dorky dressing began in the early sixties (when Arnold Palmer won the Masters wearing pants with belt loops but no belt), crested in the mid-seventies (when Hale Irwin's sideburns dipped below the stems of his glasses), and ended in the mid-eighties (when Levi-Strauss introduced Dockers). Nowadays, a golf correspondent who takes potshots at polyester is like a high-school principal who still complains that you can't tell the boys from the girls. When was the last time you bought a pair of yellow-and-brown plaid double-knit golf pants?

Nobody at my club still wears synthetic fabrics except for a few old guys, who never throw anything away and bequeath the contents of their closets to one another when they die. Their golf shirts—with pointy collars that droop so low they impede a full turn—are almost as old as their golf balls, which they dredge from the pre-Cambrian silt at the bottom of our pond. All the rest of us, though, look pretty decent, and I'm sure the same is true at your club. The only nice thing my wife has ever said about golf is that it improved my wardrobe. (I work at home, so khakis and polo shirts were a major upgrade for me.)

As a matter of fact, golf's history is mainly one of sartorial honor. In Walter Hagen's day, even the caddies tried to dress like Walter Hagen, and no athlete in action has ever been better attired than Bobby Jones in the twenties or Ben Hogan in the fifties. On the PGA Tour nowadays, there's a heck of a lot more cashmere than there is rayon. And most of the guys on the Senior Tour even wear belts a lot of the time. If anything, golf clothes are in danger of becoming too nice. (Do even rich people really want three-hundred-dollar golf shirts?) When Wall Street lawyers and investment bankers hold dress-down days at work, they dress like . . . golfers.

The only clothing category about which modern golfers need to feel ashamed is footwear. (Who invented white wingtips, and why?) Admittedly, the golf-shoe problem is a tough one. Golf is kind of like a sport—yet true sports shoes (like running shoes) look dumb sticking out from under the cuffs of regular trousers. And golf is also kind of not like a sport—yet excessively regular-looking shoes detract from the competitive atmosphere. But we can clearly do better. Not even cheerleaders wear saddle shoes anymore. So why do we?

The Law of
Maximum Irritation

I HAD A BIG GOLF GAME PLANNED for the following day. The forecast was lousy, so all afternoon I kept my TV tuned to the Weather Channel. (Obsessive viewing of the Weather Channel is the closest thing in the male golf world to an organized religion.) Every time the radar map came on, I dropped what I was doing and stared. It is sometimes possible to create a localized high-pressure system by exerting fierce mental and optical energy on particular parts of a television screen. On rare occasions, I have succeeded in diverting full-blown tropical depressions.

The following morning, I read only the sports section of the newspaper and never turned on the TV. Checking the forecast on the day of a golf game greatly increases the likelihood of rain, because rain clouds, like wild animals, can smell fear. As I left the house for the course, at eleven, my wife asked if I would be home for dinner. "I'll probably be back before lunch," I said. "It's supposed to rain hard all afternoon—why don't we plan on taking the kids to a movie?"

That was a desperate move on my part. The sky looked so dark at that moment that I had felt compelled to invoke the Law of Maximum Irritation. The law states that the likelihood of completing a given round of golf increases in direct proportion to the amount of trouble the golfer will get into when it is over. By virtually promising my wife that I would be available for a wholesome family outing in the afternoon, I came close to guaranteeing that the storm would hold off at least until *Titanic* was sold out.

As I drove to the course, the morning's sprinkles became real rain, but I never turned the wipers above intermittent speed. Running the wipers at full force encourages a storm and may promote lightning. I also put on my sunglasses and my golf glove, and I rolled down my window and stuck my elbow jauntily into the downpour.

Alas, those bold measures didn't work. In fact, the rain became more intense as I pulled into the parking lot. So, in a final heroic attempt to appease the golf gods, I threw a maiden into the volcano: I sacrificed the back nine. "Just give me nine holes!" I cried, while smiting the dashboard with my (gloved) left fist. "And rain all you want! Just hold the thunder until two-thirty!"

And that, finally, was enough. The clouds began to break up right before we teed off, and the rain stopped altogether before we made the turn—although we were careful never to take off our rainsuits or put away our umbrellas.* Of course, I was in big trouble when I finally got home, after several beers, at seven o'clock. But I didn't care. To tell you the truth, I almost always get in trouble when I play golf.

---

*Paradoxically, behavior that encourages rain before a round can help to prevent rain once the players have teed off. For similar reasons, the more expensive your rainsuit is, the less likely you are ever to need it—unless you leave it in the trunk of your car.

Short and Sweet

I HIT A DECENT DRIVE from the first tee, and Zane, our pro at the time, who had been watching from the other side of the fence, said, "You know, when you stay behind the ball, you almost always hit a good shot." That seemingly casual remark inaugurated a six-week period during which I played the most consistently good golf I've ever played. I didn't understand exactly what Zane meant by "stay behind the ball"—and I'm not sure I understand now—but his simple observation some-how reduced the vast, expanding universe of my swing flaws to a manageable singularity. "Just stay behind it," I would say to myself as I started my backswing, and, sure enough, I would almost always hit a good shot. I didn't think about my grip or my alignment or the position of my butt. I just—well, I just stayed behind the ball. Zane, after studying the hopelessly tangled skein of my golf swing, had grabbed a single dangling thread and given it a tug. It was the shortest golf lesson I ever had, and the best.

The magic eventually wore off, of course, because in golf the magic always wears off. (The catalyst in this case was a two-week family vacation during which I, trying to be a domestic hero, left my clubs at home.) But Zane later gave me another one-sentence lesson, and it was almost as good. "Instead of aiming at the flag or a point on the fairway," he said one day as I was struggling on the range, "aim at a cloud directly above it."

In both instances, I now realize, he was addressing the complex of mechanical errors which constitutes the fundamental core of my golf game: my usually irresistible urge to sway and lunge and slash over the top. But he didn't force me to study videotapes and lab tests and X rays documenting the heartbreaking scope of my problems. He kept the details of the diagnosis to himself, and distilled the cure into a metaphor.

The golf swing happens so fast, and with so little guidance from the conscious parts of the brain, that most of its elements can be shaped only indirectly. Very often, what we really do when we swing is not what we think we're doing, or even what we think we see on tape. Different teachers have different ways of describing—even different ways of seeing—the basic elements of good swings. Is it any wonder that we often get confused? The best teachers are not necessarily the ones who are able to tell us exactly what we're doing wrong; the best teachers are the ones who are able to nudge us, in ways we can accommodate, into doing what we are supposed to do.

Butch Harmon doesn't have to keep secrets from Tiger Woods, who, in addition to everything else, is blessed with a sort of internal Global Positioning System, which keeps him constantly aware of the whereabouts of every muscle fiber in his body. But I wouldn't be able to cope with even a fraction of that information. Without a comfortably high level of ignorance about myself, I'm pretty sure, I wouldn't be able to play at all.

Golf and Communism

GOLF, LIKE ALL SPORTS, is perfectly meritocratic: If you shoot the best score, you win. At the same time, though, golf is highly socialistic. In fact, it's the world's only welfare state that works: The U.S.G.A.'s handicapping system takes strokes from each according his ability and gives them to each according to his need—communism with a human face. Unlike raw capitalism, golf has figured out how to foster individual achievement without smothering the hopes of those who can't keep up. Like most golfers, I am proud to give strokes yet unashamed to receive them.

You'd think that a system designed to facilitate gambling among strangers would be fatally vulnerable to inconsistencies and abuses. In fact, though, the handicapping system, like the post office, works better than we have any right to expect. I often play nassaus with people I don't know—people whose ideas about reportable scores may differ wildly from my own—and yet far more often than the laws of probability would predict, our matches come down to the final press or the final hole or the final putt. How does that happen?

The explanation, I think, is that human nature makes the handicap system almost magically self-correcting. A golfer with a pop has a mindset different from that of a golfer playing naked. Players with too many strokes inevitably find ways to waste them, and players with too few are often inspired to shoot better than they know how. (Ben Hogan—or was it Sam Snead?—once played a match with an amateur who complained that he wasn't receiving enough strokes, and Snead—or was it Gene Sarazen?—replied, "Then you're just going to have to play harder.") Every club has its sandbaggers, chiselers, pretenders, and poseurs, but, over the course of a season or two, the bets tend to even out. One way or another most of us manage to live up, or down, to our innermost expectations.

Despite its genius, though, the handicapping system is not the only possible tool for leveling matches between unequal players. I have studied this matter as carefully as Trotsky studied Marx, and I have uncovered some attractive alternatives.

The simplest, conceptually, is the Shout, first described, I believe, by Henry Longhurst. Instead of giving a less-skilled opponent three strokes, for example, a better player might offer one shout. At any point during the match, that is, the opponent would be entitled to emit one blood-curdling scream—say, at the top of the better player's backswing. The key to successful shouting is to continually seem to be on the verge of doing it—perhaps by inhaling audibly as the better player takes the club back—without actually using it up.

A less publicly disruptive instrument for equalizing a golf

match is the Reverse Mulligan. A player entitled to an R.M. can require an opponent to replay any shot in the round. Let's say the better player miraculously sinks a double-breaking eight-foot sidehill putt, or hits a drive three hundred yards dead straight down the center of the course's tightest fairway, or sinks a long blast from the sand. The less-skilled opponent effusively praises the shot, then says, "I'd like to see that again."

A more complex adjustment is the Radical Clubectomy, in which the inferior player is allowed, on the first tee, to remove an agreed-upon number of clubs from the better player's bag. If granted a triple clubectomy, for example, the inferior player might grab the better player's driver, sand wedge, and put-ter—or, more deviously, might instead remove three of the driver's less temperamental alternatives, such as the three-wood, the five-wood, and the three-iron.

All three of these handicap alternatives are intended to narrow the skill gap by hobbling the better player. But one can also approach the problem from the opposite direction, by granting an advantage to the laggard. At *Golf Digest* staff out-ings, for example, it has sometimes been customary to offer high-handicap players "a throw a side," in addition to their regular allotment of strokes. A player with a throw is allowed, once per nine holes, to throw his ball toward its target instead of attempting to strike it with a club. Players most often use their throws to extricate themselves from sand traps, but other applications are possible. One of the magazine's editors once won an important match by using his throw to sink a crucial eight-foot putt on the final hole. He stood behind his ball marker, lifted his ball high above his head, fell forward, and slam-dunked his ball into the hole just before his face struck the turf.

Any of these devices may be used in combination with any other, and with regular handicaps as well. "I'll give you six strokes, one shout, and two throws," a scratch player might offer you. And you might counter, "How about five strokes, one throw, one reverse mulligan, and you leave your pitching wedge in your car?" Even behind golf's iron curtain, negotiation is a part of the game.

My Scratch Index

MY ONLY SERIOUS QUIBBLE with the U.S.G.A.'s handicapping system (or with the four alternatives, or supplements, to it that I just proposed) is that its outlook is essentially negative. For the vast majority of us, a handicap is a gauge of inadequacy—a measure of the distance by which we fall short. It's an index of our flaws, not of our strengths.

Lately, I've tried to think of my game from the other direction, and to help me do that I've devised a new scale, which I call the Scratch Index. My Scratch Index is the mirror image of my handicap index. It's a measure of how close I come to playing the game the way I wish I were able to play it.

My Scratch Index is the number of holes in a typical round over which I manage to maintain a running score of even par. The holes don't have to be consecutive. If I make nine pars, one birdie, five bogeys, and three doubles, as I did on a recent Sunday, then my Scratch Index for that round is eleven—because the birdie plus one of the bogeys equals two pars, and adding those two pars to the other nine makes eleven. For eleven out of eighteen holes, in other words, I played like a scratch player. That means that just seven bad holes stand between me and a round of even par—not bad!

My Scratch Index wouldn't be very useful as a tool for leveling a match between me and somebody else. But that's not what it's for. It's a personal measure, by which I keep track of my progress, or my decline, as a player. It's a comforting number, because it accentuates the positive. In that way, it's a little like a ringer score, which is an eighteen-hole score made up of a player's best-ever performance on each of a course's holes. I played Pebble Beach three times one week in 1994. My best round (by far) was an 82—but my three-round ringer score was even par.

Realistically, I know I'll never be a scratch player. But thinking about my Scratch Index reminds me that I have a pretty good idea of what being a scratch player would feel like. After all, on that recent Sunday, I played like one two-thirds of the time.

Golf Is a Game
of Giving Up

I WAS PLAYING AN IMPORTANT MATCH with a golfer from another club. I was swinging well, and I had my opponent on the ropes—or so it seemed. Every half-baked solution he tried—swinging harder, swinging easier, teeing off with irons instead of woods—merely made his problems worse. Finally, when I had him three down with four to go, the look of anguished intensity vanished from his eyes, and I could tell that he had given up.

"Uh-oh," I thought.

I was right. As soon as he stopped caring, his drives straightened out, his wedge became a weapon, and his putts began to drop. He won three holes in a row with two birdies and a par, and, before either of us had fully comprehended what had happened, our match was all square.

"Whew," I thought.

Once again, I was right. Suddenly realizing that victory, against all odds, was within his grasp, my opponent began to care again, and his swing promptly imploded. I myself had been floundering at that point, having watched with growing horror as my lead slipped away—but I had just about resigned myself to the inevitability of a humiliating defeat, and, therefore, the tension in my arms was gradually dissolving. Thus composed, I was able to scramble for a double-bogey on the final hole, beating my opponent's triple. The match was mine.

Despair has the same relaxing effect on a golf swing that self-assurance does, and it's far easier for most of us to come by: Hopelessness is the poor man's confidence. The most dangerous player in match play is the one who has mentally surrendered, because conscientious effort is the gremlin that destroys a chopper's swing. We all play better when we play alone, because when no one is looking and nothing is at stake we ourselves stop paying attention. As soon as the outcome begins to matter to us, though, we go back to getting in our own way.

Beware of the golfer who has given up. Study your opponent closely, and blow gently on the embers of his hopes the first time he fails to slam his driver back into his bag. Keep him focused on the match. Don't let him stop to smell the roses, and, whatever you do, don't let his thoughts drift forward to the post-round beers. Praise his putting stroke. Compliment the sweeping arc of his banana. Never for a moment let him think that he no longer has a chance.

Mrs. Murphy

ON VACATION WITH MY FAMILY in Florida one winter, I managed to qualify for my wife's stringent Golf Release program. I had done four days of hard time at two beaches, a nature preserve, a G-rated movie, and a seashell museum, and as a reward I had been granted eighteen holes of unsupervised play on the golf course at the resort where we were staying. (That we were staying at a resort with a course was proof that this was a minimum-security vacation, but I nonetheless had had to earn my round.) At noon, I walked out of the door of our villa wearing my favorite golf shirt, which hadn't seen natural light since early October. For the next six hours I was, relatively speaking, a free man.

I had no trouble securing a tee time on short notice. Even at a crowded resort, you can be certain that, at least once per hour, some golfing husband with a tee time will violate the terms of his parole and be returned to family confinement, creating an opening for a single. The only problem is that you, as an unattached player, invariably end up playing with strangers, whose handicaps are of uncertain provenance, and often in less than a full foursome. So how do you gamble?

That was the dilemma I faced in Florida. The starter grouped me with two dentists from Ohio. (They were supposed to be playing with friends from home, but the missing pair had been captured the night before in an ill-considered alcohol-related escape attempt and were now being held in solitary.) Fortunately, my father had taught me the perfect game for just this situation. It's called Mrs. Murphy.

In my dad's game, you turn a threesome into a foursome by adding an imaginary fourth player, named Mrs. Murphy. She's a kindly old Irish grandmother, who wears a big hat and a long skirt, and she can't hit the ball more than a hundred and thirty yards, but she still manages to shoot par on every hole. Either that, or she's a thirtyish, recently divorced former Victoria's Secret model, who took up the game just a couple of years ago and is kind of shaky on long putts but still manages to shoot par on every hole. Your choice.

Each of the three non-imaginary players gets Mrs. Murphy as a partner in one six-hole best-ball match against the other two, who play as a team, and everybody plays off her handicap, which is zero. The key to doing well is to take advantage of Mrs. Murphy's rock-steady play during the six holes when she is your partner, by aggressively gunning for net birdies, since she's already covered par. Your opponents, meanwhile, have to play carefully enough to match Mrs. Murphy, while looking for reasonable opportunities to score.

Sandbagging questions are moot, and wide handicap spreads don't matter, since everybody gets everybody else as a partner for six holes.

Mrs. Murphy is a good game for three people, no matter where you are or who you're playing with, and competing against par is a useful teaching aid under any circumstances. I had a big smile on my face that evening in Florida when I returned to our villa, a few minutes before my curfew, and the warden led me back to my cell.

Winter Rules

D URING THE FIRST AND LAST DAYS of every playing season, when our course is sodden and overgrown, my regular golf buddies and I permit ourselves to lift, clean, and creatively place our balls within a club-length of where we find them, even in bunkers. I used to fret about this brazen violation of the game's official rules; golf's most sacred imperative, after all, is "play the ball as it lies." But I've stopped feeling bad about rolling them over. As my friend Tim said recently, "There's a genuine art to improving a lie."

Adopting so-called winter rules creates shotmaking opportunities that few of us would otherwise experience. There's a par-five on my course which I have little chance of reaching in two—unless I've sliced my drive into the weedy wasteland to the right of the fairway and perched my ball on the crest of a tee-like tuft of desiccated scrub, so that I can smack it with my driver. Nestling my ball down slightly in the dry nap of a shaggy winter fairway makes my six-iron shots fly far and straight. After rolling my ball onto a patch of frost-burned turf, even I can produce backspin with my wedges. Fluffing up the rough on the brink of a greenside bunker enables me to hit parabolic flop shots, just like Tiger. Once, taking maximum advantage of my one-club radius of relief, I positioned myself in the gap between two low branches and used my three-wood to punch my ball from a mound of pine needles all the way to the front edge of the green, a distance of two hundred yards.

Golf courses would be cheaper to maintain if we all played all the time by winter rules. Fairways wouldn't have to be manicured; in fact, wildly inconsistent playing conditions would be prized, because they would offer the broadest spectrum of exploitable lies. (A worm cast makes a handy natural tee.) The most common forms of casual cheating would be neutralized, since the guys who now depend on foot-wedges would lose their competitive advantage. Divot holes and clumps of mud would cease to matter. Equipment manufacturers would thrive, as players rethought their choice of clubs. (How about a huge-headed wedge for plucking a ball from the peak of a carefully molded cone of bunker sand?)

Of course, we would lose something as well. Playing golf with preferred lies is like playing poker with wild cards: real royal flushes are devalued when threes and nines are wild. For most of us, though, the gain would more than offset the loss. There's something thrilling about launching a big banana from the tee and shouting, "Get in the rough!"

Going Cross Country

Merion, Oakmont, Pebble Beach, and Pine Valley—courses that perennially inhabit the uppermost decile of *Golf Digest*'s biennial ranking of the hundred best golf courses in America—have a surprising common feature: all four were designed by novices. The architects were regular guys who had never attended a graduate seminar in bunker theory. None knew much about course design; each just knew what he liked.

The amateur era ended long ago, of course; the youngest of those four courses was finished in the 1920s. Nowadays, not even Donald Trump would have the chutzpah to do what George Crump did in 1912, when he sold a hotel he owned in Philadelphia, bought a huge tract of scrub land in southern New Jersey, and, with very little help from anyone else, laid out most of Pine Valley—which today is widely regarded as the best course in the world. Crump's principal design tool was innocently uncomplicated: he hit golf shots into the weeds, and built greens where the good ones ended up.

Yet if Crump could do it, why not someone else? Why not (even) Trump?

I myself often think about course design in the cold months of the year. Every Saturday and Sunday during the long winter, my most golf-obsessed friends and I meet on the first tee of our club, which is otherwise closed for the duration, and make up a new golf course.

We do a pretty good job, and the work isn't as hard as you might think—even though we face constraints no architect ever did. Our greens (all temporaries) are already in place, and we can't move dirt or fell trees. Also, the entire course is often buried under snow. But we don't feel limited. Creating a good hole is less a matter of construction than of imagination. Our summer course—which covers just forty acres—turns out to contain many excellent winter courses. Now that we've trained ourselves to see the holes, we could play a dozen rounds without repeating.

We take turns at the drawing board. "Over the trees to the sixth fairway," someone says, "then across the creek to the bottom of the eighth and up to the temporary second green. Par-five." Long hitters play over the trees; old-timers look for gaps between the branches. My favorite hole is the fourth played backward, to the temporary green on three. Instead of driving over a pond to the base of a steep hill, you drive over the crest of the hill and try to make your ball run down the frozen fairway to the edge of the pond. From there, you have to play a high shot over a creek to a flag that's tucked behind two trees. Then it's someone else's turn to choose.

Sometimes, Bob joins us. Standing on the fourth tee one Sunday, he said, "O.K., the pond is the green. If your ball rolls off, you're out." The pond, which lies about a hundred and fifty yards from the tee, was frozen a foot thick, and the ice was black and slicker than the slickest green on Sunday at Augusta. I hit a high fade into the snow on the near shore, and my ball just trickled on. Another time, we pretended that the flag was the left-hand marker on the lower tee on four, just beyond the pond, forcing a player to land his approach shot on the ice and bounce it up over the bank.

Six of the nine regular holes on our golf course are crossed by a single yard-wide stream, which runs from west to east across the lowest contour of the club's property. Some of my favorite winter holes run parallel to that stream, and therefore perpendicular to the heart of our course—such as a par-three that runs from the women's back tee on the fourth hole to a parking-space-sized shelf of fairway at the bottom of the hill below the second green. If you hit that landing area, you feel like Tiger Woods; if your ball finds the water instead, the stream carries it back toward you as you walk to fetch it, like the ball return at a bowling alley.

Snow Golf

SOMETIMES WHEN MY FRIENDS and I play cross-country golf in the winter, our course is covered with snow. When it is, we play with orange or pink balls—unless the snow is so deep that color becomes irrelevant, in which case we sometimes use white. When the sun is bright and the snow is deep, we track our shots by sound as much as by sight. Someone aims into the glare while everyone else stands still with one ear pointed down the fairway, waiting for a muffled thump. Then we trudge in what we hope is the right direction. We play to the flags in the winter cups, just short of the real greens. Hitting the pin counts as holing out. Reluctantly, we share the course with cross-country skiers, whose tracks and pole marks complicate the art of rescuing our shots. Deer footprints are a nuisance, too. We try to aim for unspoiled patches, so that the holes our balls make will be easier to find.

You don't need all your clubs when you play in the snow. My friends and I usually carry just a six-iron or a seven-iron. Playing with one club forces you to become a shotmaker, because virtually every shot you face is either too long or too short for the implement in your hand. I now know how to get extra distance over icy ground by closing the club face and moving the ball back in my stance. And I know how to hit a fluffy explosion shot out of a snow bank by laying the head of the club practically flat.

Dressing for snow golf is a challenge. The idea is to add warmth without muffling your swing. I wear several layers of sweaters so that I can peel them off as the steep hills heat me up. Surprisingly, I find that I often swing better with a couple of sweaters on, because the extra bulk keeps my arms and elbows from flying out of orbit. The great Harry Vardon used to say that every golfer should play in a jacket and suspenders, as he did, to keep the swing compact.

My friend Dick, who seldom takes a waking breath that isn't filtered through a cheap cigar, wears heavy rubber boots that go up almost to his knees. He calls them sheep boots, for a reason I won't repeat. I wear steel-toed leather clodhoppers with Vibram soles. They grip the ground so firmly that I would wear them during the regular season, too, except that Bob would dump me in the pond if he ever saw me thumping across his greens.

One winter, after a couple of big storms had dumped four feet of snow in a single week, I bought a pair of snowshoes specifically for golf. Before teeing off that weekend, my friends and I surveyed the course from above the uppermost rail of the fence behind the first tee; we could just see the tops of the fence posts sticking out of the white. Snowshoes would make a useful teaching aid in any weather: they keep your feet securely planted, forcing you to coil your backswing around a firm right leg. They are also useful for tamping down teeing areas, a necessity in deep powder.

Golf in the snow is not better than golf on grass; I am never sorry to see the winter end. But because I have tramped my course in snowshoes, spring means more to me than it does to my friends who escape to Florida when the weather turns cold. When you've played your course in a blizzard, you don't forget that golf in any season is a gift.

You May Be a Winner

My friend Tony gave a golf trip to his son one Christmas. And Tony's son gave a golf trip to his uncle. And the uncle gave a golf trip to Tony. As these gifts were revealed, one by one, over the course of Christmas morning, Tony's mother-in-law's astonishment grew. "I can't believe you all gave each other a vacation to the same place! And on the same weekend!"

Not all non-golfers are as easy to fool as Tony's mother-in-law was. A gambit like that would never work with my wife, for example, because she knows (and is appalled) that my brother and I long ago agreed to simplify our lives by never giving each other anything for any reason. Tony's wife wasn't fooled, either, but she said nothing, because the men of the family had (astutely) expressed their selfishness in a form that seemed to endorse a deeply cherished belief held by the women of the family: that major holidays are important occasions for loving commitment and renewal, and so forth. The men got what they wanted by pretending to play the game by the women's rules.

Anyway, Tony's success at Christmas got me thinking, and I'm pretty sure I've come up with an even better idea. My idea is so good, in fact, that I'm going to share it with you.

Here's what I've done. I've started a company called the International Golf Sweepstakes Foundation, Inc., of which I am the sole employee. Let's say that you and three buddies want to take a ten-day golf trip to Ireland, but you know that your wives would never in a million years let you go. You contact me by e-mail, and I send you an entry form for a contest in which the grand prize happens to be an all-expenses-paid ten-day golf trip to Ireland for four. You fill out the form and ask your wife to sign her name on the line marked "witness."

"What's this?" she asks.

"Oh, just some dumb animal-rights thing they made us contribute to at work."

Your wife happily signs, you send the form back to me with a check for five hundred dollars (my fee), and you never again mention the contest to your wife. Three or four months later, a fat, official-looking FedEx package arrives at your house. You open it in the presence of your wife, appear puzzled for a moment, then begin hooting. "Remember that dumb contest?" you shout. "I actually won!"

Non-playing wives view all golf trips as wasteful extravagances, but they can't help thinking of contest winnings as money in the bank. To fail to cash in a prize already won would be like throwing jewelry out in the trash, so of course you'll get to go—especially if you promptly offer to give your wife some sort of compensating goodie, like a new kitchen. You'll have to make all your travel arrangements yourself—and conceal your credit card charges as you do—because that's not part of what my foundation does, at least for the time being. All I do is get you out the door. The rest is up to you.

Waiting for Spring

My wife hates it when I tee off before nine on weekend mornings. If I push my first shot, the ball ricochets off the wall, slips through the balusters, and clatters down the stairs. That makes the dogs think someone is at the door, so they jump onto the back of the couch and bark at the window. Meanwhile, I'm trying to gather my composure for a delicate lob to the second floor. The rug by our front door is an old Oriental, and parts of it are worn almost bare. If I sway even slightly—an old problem of mine—I blade the ball dead into the bottom riser and it pops back against my feet: two strokes. That's generally when my wife appears at the top of the stairs and makes various angry remarks. I might as well take an X right there and go on to the second hole.

Don't get me wrong—I like playing indoors. But there are times when it hardly seems worth the trouble. I'm tired of explaining to my kids why they aren't allowed to eat in the living room, but it's O.K. for me to hit knocked-down nine-irons into the chairs. I don't remember ever being quite so rude to my own parents. Meanwhile, my wife thinks I should confine my indoor playing to the basement and my office, or at least not start until she's awake—even though the basement isn't carpeted, my office is too small for anything but chips and putts, and I hate letting half the morning slip away while I wait for her to get up.

A possible compromise would be for me to switch to foam-rubber balls, at least for tee shots. But what would that do to my feel? Granted, I can't take full swings anyway: our ceilings are so low that I am constantly in danger of damaging my clubs. But I think it's important to maintain some connection with reality, and partial shots with real balls help you groove the bottom quarter of your arc. When our course finally reopens, I don't want to show up on the first tee with swing thoughts derived from hitting marshmallows. Golf is hard enough as it is.

Putting is the one part of my game I'm not worried about. The carpet in my office rolls at 8.5 on the Stimpmeter—not fast by tournament standards, but pretty good for level-loop pile. Our house is more than two hundred years old, so there's plenty of break, especially near my desk. I've been able to vir-tually eliminate grain, by vacuuming monodirectionally and being careful not to drag my feet. For targets, I use paperclips or dimes, on the theory that smaller is better. A real hole would be nice in some ways, but cutting through the floor would raise the potentially thorny issue of inter-joist ball retrieval.

Oh, when will it be spring?

On Becoming
a Woodsman

O<small>N A GOLF TRIP</small> down South one winter, I handed one of my fairway woods to the professional at the course where I was playing. "Hit a few shots with this," I said, "but don't look at the sole plate." He hit four long, high, perfect draws.

"Now look," I said.

He looked. The club I had given him was my eleven-wood, which had recently taken the place of the five-iron in my bag. His jaw dropped.

"Now try this one," I said. I handed him my nine-wood. He hit four long, high, perfect draws.

He tried my seven-wood, too.

"Shit," he said when he had finished. "Why does anybody carry a goddamned iron?" That afternoon, he got rid of his long irons and replaced them with woods, bringing the total in his bag to five. (He now carries all the odd-numbered woods from the driver through the nine-wood, and his longest iron is a five.) Back on the driving range again, he made one of his assistants stand in the middle of the landing area with a laser range-finder, so he could determine exactly how far he hit each of his new clubs. Then he went back into his shop and bent his five-iron a degree or two stronger, to narrow a gap he had discovered between that club and his nine-wood.

I'm not a pro, so I usually carry six woods instead of just five. My regular golf buddies think it's hilarious that my longest iron is a six-iron. But I don't care. If I could find a thirteen-wood, I'd get rid of my six-iron, too. (At the Masters one year, I asked Callaway Golf's chief club designer why his company didn't sell a thirteen-wood, and he explained that, among other things, such a club would have so much loft that it would be in danger of sliding right under a ball.)

Many teaching pros still view even seven-woods only as "utility" clubs—novelty implements of no utility to anyone except old guys, ten-year-olds, beginners, and wives. The pros don't have trouble with their long irons, so they don't understand the appeal. Most new sets of golf clubs still include three-irons—even though most regular golfers would get more use from a second umbrella. The professional bias against high-numbered woods is so strong that if you decide tomorrow that you want to own an eleven-wood, you'll probably have to order it.

I know a couple of driver-impaired high-handicappers who have gotten pretty good at hitting a two-iron off a tee. But they are hopeless at hitting even a five-iron off the ground, and most of them use their three-iron only to chip balls out from under trees. (When I told a slashing friend of mine that I had sworn off long irons, he asked, sincerely, "What do you use in the blue spruces?") Like almost all of us, they develop too little club-head speed and have too little eye-hand coordination to make consistently decent shots with long irons, which are fiendishly unforgiving. They keep at it because they think there's something shameful about owning more than three head covers.

I've heard all kinds of excuses: a nine-wood hits the ball too high, a seven-wood hits the ball too far, you can't back up a shot with an eleven-wood, practicing with a three-iron makes a seven-iron seem easy.

But high and far are assets in golf, nobody I know can back up a five-iron, either, and the best way to make a seven-iron seem easy is to practice with a seven-iron. If you want proof that high-numbered fairway woods are worth more than mere "utility," watch an LPGA Tour event on TV sometime. Annika Sorenstam carries pretty much the same selection of clubs that I do, as do many other female pros. The fact that they can't swing a two-iron as fast as Tiger can doesn't mean they're bad players.

A couple of months after performing my eleven-wood demonstration down South, I tried the same trick on my pro at home. "Gee," Fran said after hitting half a dozen perfect shots. "Maybe I ought to sell these things."

That's a start. Before too long, I'll have him playing with them, too.

Playing It Safe

Recently, a man I know took his family skiing. I had deep misgivings about the vacation. Having spent some time in mountains many years before, I knew that skiers face an inordinate risk of golf-threatening injury. Sure enough, when my friend returned, he was hobbling. He had torn some cartilage in one knee. The prognosis for his swing was uncertain.

When my father was seventy, he slipped on an icy step while carrying bird seed to his feeder. He shattered an ankle and never played a full round again; a few years later, in fact, he cleaned out his locker at his club and shipped all his old equipment to my son, who was just beginning to play. (My son sold all my dad's stuff on eBay and used the proceeds to outfit himself with clubs that didn't seem quite so geriatric.) There are those who say the game has been enriched by my father's absence from it. He, understandably, has a different view. He never dreamed, as he headed out the door with a bag of millet slung over his shoulder, that he had played his last eighteen.

A couple of years ago, my friend Ed stumbled on the steep back stairs of his house while carrying his mother's suitcase to her car. Before he fell, he was probably thinking, "Mother leaving—good—more time for golf." He sprained an elbow, broke both shoulder blades, cracked a couple of ribs, and fractured an obscure bone at the base of his spine. His injuries were so severe that he could think of no persuasive rejoinder when his wife suggested that he drop his membership at our club. Not long ago, after months of therapy, he joined me for a tentative round. I beat him seven ways.

Skiing, bird-feeding, and helping one's parents are not the only activities that prudent golfers must avoid. Bungee jumping, fighting in wars, leaping from speeding trains, playing football, dancing, running, lifting small children, sitting anywhere in a theater except near an exit, shopping, eating undercooked food, and mowing the lawn are all incompatible with a life devoted to golf. The risk of swing-debilitating injury is simply too great.

I know a golfer who once had a traffic accident, so lately I've been thinking about giving up my car. When I need to get to the golf course, I'll call a cab and lie across the backseat wearing all three seatbelts while reminding the driver to use seldom-traveled roads and stay well below the speed limit. Not driving will be inconvenient, but not playing would be worse. Or maybe I should just live at the club—something my wife has accused me of doing anyway.

The potential threats to golf, once you think to look for them, are everywhere. Possibly vicious animals roam free in the suburbs. Hurricanes are hard to predict and impossible to control. Airplanes routinely fly over inhabited areas. Even golf itself can be golf-threatening. A woman at my club wrenched her back while trying to make a movement she had read about in a monthly golf publication; now she can't bend over to tee up a ball.

A few more yards off the tee, a few giddy moments on a snow-covered slope—how important would those fleeting pleasures seem if you could no longer play at all?

Secret of the Swing

I DISCOVERED THE SECRET of the golf swing one afternoon. All I have to do is shift my—well, it's too complicated to explain. But the secret enables me to hit the ball high and straight and long.

Actually, discovering the secret of the golf swing is an old thing with me: I do it every year toward the end of the golf season. On some chilly afternoon in mid-November, I try something new out of desperation—maybe turn my grip another knuckle, or open or close my stance, or lean a little to the right (or left) at address—and the change solves all my problems, immediately.

Then the first snow falls, and our course shuts down, and I put my clubs away until spring. I'm not sad that the season has ended, though. Knowing that I know the secret of the golf swing keeps my hopes alive all winter long. I practice the secret in front of the mirror. I rehearse the new movement in my mind. I think about it when I'm supposed to be working. And I daydream about all the terrific golf I'm going to play as soon as my club reopens.

When spring finally does arrive, I take my secret to the course and, to the astonishment of my friends, it works beautifully. "I've never seen you hit the ball better," my buddy Ray or Rick or Tony says. "Did you go to golf school over the winter?" That lasts for nine or ten holes, or maybe for a round or two. Then the secret stops working, and I turn back into my old crummy self. No matter how hard I try to recapture the magic I discovered the year before, my flawless new swing is gone.

It happens every spring. Why?

Well, I've been watching *E.R.* reruns and reading some medical journals online, and I've developed a hypothesis. Here it is: The bodies of average golfers cannot tolerate extended periods of good golf.

Good golf swings are like viruses, I've determined. When we hit good shots, our immune system identifies our swing as a deadly intruder and mobilizes to destroy it. Antibodies rush into our bloodstream, our swing thoughts become confused, and our ability to metabolize alcohol is undermined.

Some good golf swings survive longer than others. That's because some swings, like some pathogens, are difficult for our bodies to eradicate. (Practice swings, lay-up shots, and provisional balls don't seem to be affected at all.) But our bodies always prevail, especially when our new swing has been weakened by competition, pressed bets, or a better player.

Why aren't good players affected by any of this? They are, to some degree. But good players, by definition, are players who are inordinately susceptible to benevolent infection. Their immune system has been compromised. When a good swing contaminates their golf game, they are powerless to eradicate it. That helps their scoring, but it leaves them dangerously vulnerable to a host of illnesses, such as braggadocio, hubris, and tumescent self-esteem.

Don't envy low handicappers. Feel sorry for them. They are very, very sick.

Scrambling in Reverse

ON EVENINGS IN THE SPRING, when our course has yet to be rediscovered by most of the members of our club, my friend Ray and I sometimes play a game that we call a one-man reverse scramble. We each hit two balls from the first tee, then each play two second shots from the worse of our two drives, and so on, until we have both holed out. If there is ever a doubt about which of any pair of shots is stinkier, the opposing player gets to choose. (Plugged in the bunker, or stymied behind the tree? Hmmm.) The game forces us to restrain our early-season enthusiasm and search for swings that have at least a slight chance of working more than one time in a row. Smoothness and consistency are the keys, because every good first shot is subject to immediate downward revision by a crummy second.

Ray and I didn't make up our game all by ourselves; we were inspired by the Canadian ball-striking legend Moe Norman, who sometimes entertains himself late in the day by playing the worst of four balls over nine holes. Norman once told me that he has occasionally managed to shoot a nine-hole score of even par or better in that format—a mind-boggling achievement, given the tendency of even small errors to compound themselves under forced repetition, especially on greens. Ray and I are happy if we end up making no more than what seems like a reasonable number of triple bogeys.

We were also inspired by a match I once played with Fran, our pro, who was then our assistant. I was helping him prepare to compete in a PGA-sponsored tournament, in which his score would determine whether or not he advanced to the next level in his career. To even our match, and to put some extra pressure on him, we decided that we would each hit two drives from every tee, and that he would have to play the worse of his two drives while I would get to play the better of mine. Surprisingly, this arrangement had a more salutary effect on his score than it did on mine. While he concentrated on keeping his swing steady and smooth, to increase his likelihood of being left with a reasonable second shot, I would try to hit a safe bloop single with my first drive and then swing out of my shoes. After a few holes, I lost track of my shoes.

Reverse-scrambling is good for a full swing, but it's lousy for a putting stroke. "Make it twice" is the last thing your brain wants to hear if you're standing over a curling four-footer that will win the hole. What Ray and I really ought to do, in the interest of grooming our games, is to change formats once we reach the green, and give ourselves a free do-over on every putt. I've never been a better putter than I was in a silly tournament in which each player was granted one floating mulligan, which could be used at any point in the round. I forgot about mine for fifteen holes, then never had a chance to use it, because simply knowing that it was in my pocket enabled me to one-putt the last three greens. "We don't need to make this one," I told my brain as I stood over those final three putts. So of course they all went in.

The Big C

As I DROVE HOME from my dermatologist's office, I felt more than slightly annoyed. Slicing two unsightly bumps from the side of my nose had taken the doctor roughly eleven seconds, from Novocain to Band-Aid, yet had cost me more than a thousand dollars. With five minutes of instruction, I figured, I could have performed the operation myself, using tools I already own. But I calmed down a few weeks later, when I went back for a follow-up appointment. One of the bumps was just a harmless old-guy surface enigma, the doctor said. The other, though, was something I really did need a licensed physician to deal with: a basal cell carcinoma—skin cancer.

Golfers face an elevated risk of developing all sorts of skin trouble—especially golfers who, like me, grew up in the pre-sunscreen era, when kids were pretty much expected to broil away the top few layers of their epidermis every summer. Lounging by the pool at the country club, my pals and I used to bet Cokes on who could peel off the largest intact sheet of stomach skin. Most of the sun-related products that people used in those days were intended not to prevent the damage caused by solar radiation but to exacerbate it. Kids who didn't appear to have been roasted and flayed were assumed to be sickly.

I followed my childhood misadventures with plenty of other bonehead moves: falling asleep on a beach in Mexico during spring break in college; working without a shirt all summer on the lawn crew at a condominium complex in Colorado; burning my nose virtually to the cartilage while covering my first professional golf tournament. ("You're in trouble, son," a tour official told me.) And although I've been less negligent about protecting myself in recent years, I have many telltale signs of overexposure, including feet that look like replacement parts because they're so much paler than the legs above my sock line. (A teenager who works as a lifeguard told me that she can always spot the golf dads at the pool: pale forehead, dark V-shaped patch of turkey skin below the throat, untanned glove hand, feet like little booties.)

A few days after my bumps were removed, I showed up at the golf course with a pair of small bandages on my nose. The bandages attracted comment, and I was partly comforted and partly appalled to learn how many other members of my small club had suffered various skin cancers, most of them more troubling than mine. Friends showed me galaxies of scars on their arms, foreheads, faces, ears, and bald spots. Three current members and one former member had even been treated for melanoma, the hydrogen bomb of dermatological problems. One of the current members had lost most of one calf in an operation to remove her tumor; the former member had received 140 stitches in his stomach. All four are still alive, though—unlike a guy I knew in high school, who was too late in discovering the asymmetrical, irregularly bordered, unevenly colored, large-diameter mole lurking in the folds of his belly button.

Several years ago, feeling mildly anxious about the sun, I bought and happily wore a golf hat with a very broad brim. One day, another golfer asked me, "Where'd you get the hat—Old Sturbridge Village?" and I threw it away. Now I'm in the market for a floor-length sombrero, and I've bought several gallons of two different kinds of sunscreen, which I apply in succession. I can't undo the damage I've already done to myself, but I'm hoping I can slow the rate at which I pay the price.

How to Putt

FROM THE WINDOW of my office, on the third floor of my house, I spotted a U.P.S. truck turning in to my driveway. The truck was delivering a new golf club, which I had bought with points I'd earned by charging my children's tuition on my credit card. I ran down the stairs two steps at a time and met the U.P.S. man halfway up the walk.

After opening the box right there and hitting a dozen shag balls into my neighbor's yard, I reflected on my trip down the stairs. Although I had run at full speed without consciously paying attention to what I was doing, I hadn't broken my neck or even stumbled. The unconscious parts of my brain, apparently, knew so much about my feet, my legs, the stairs, the banister, the wall, the floor, my hands, my running speed, the force of gravity, and so forth that I was able to make the entire trip on autopilot.

Hurling through space at full speed is not the only complicated series of actions I can perform without thinking. I can also brush my teeth while reading the newspaper, find my glasses on my bedside table in the dark, tie my shoes while watching *Golf Central*, and use my right hand to change radio stations without causing my left hand to steer my car into a bridge.

The unconscious parts of my brain are so smart, in fact, that I wonder why I don't make more use of them in golf. I blow my nose without deliberately thinking about the mechanics of nose-blowing. Why don't I putt without worrying where a golf ball would land if I dropped it from the bridge of my nose?

If you obsessively watch old golf films on the Golf Channel, as I do, you know that an awful lot of great players in the olden days employed putting methods that were, by modern standards, terrible: they stabbed at the ball instead of stroking it, allowed their wrists to bend, failed to maintain the triangle of their arms and shoulders, did not make a smooth pendulum-style motion, looked up to watch the ball rolling toward the hole, and neglected to keep the club head moving down the line.

Those old guys clearly knew nothing about putting. And yet they managed to drain an awful lot of putts. Could their secret have been that they focused on something other than mechanics? Like, maybe, the hole?

I'm willing to believe that keeping my head still and maintaining a firm left wrist are probably good ideas. But there are limits to the usefulness of conscious technique. Can sinking a four-foot putt possibly be more complicated than running down two flights of stairs?

Playing
Out of Your Mind

IN THE SAME WAY that dessert goes to a different stomach, provisional shots come from a different brain. A moment ago, you lashed a boomerang across two fairways, over the snack shack, into the trees, and probably out-of-bounds. Now, having abandoned all hope, you fish a range ball from the bottom of your bag and crease it up the center of the fairway, twenty yards past the drive of the lowest-handicap player in your foursome.

The difference between the two shots is simple. In making the first, you were trying; in making the second, you weren't. The first shot was the product of three million years of human evolution; the second was pure ape.

Lay-up shots work the same way. I usually hit my seven-iron between a hundred and fifty and a hundred and sixty yards—unless I'm laying up in front of a pond a hundred and seventy yards away, in which case I average one-seventy-five. With no thought in mind except advancing my ball down the fairway, I turn off the parts of my nervous system that got me into college and hit the ball better than I know how.

Imprisoned in every crummy golfer a good one is wildly signaling to be let out. Usually, we ignore the signals. The good golfer pops into view only on those occasions—provisional shots, lay-ups, practice swings—when we drop our guard. Invite an average golfer to hit a bucket of balls into that yawning bunker over there, and he'll miss it with every club in his bag; stick a green behind the bunker and tell him to aim at the flag, and he'll hit the sand every time.

Golf would be an easier game for dogs than it is for people; dogs wouldn't brood about bad shots. Kick your dog in the rear end for chewing up your wallet, and two minutes later he'll be licking your hand and trying to climb into your lap. If you could carry that attitude onto a golf course, you'd be unbeatable. After hitting a drive into the woods, you'd go bounding joyfully into the trees to look for your ball, nosing among the leaves, sniffing every bush, as happy as if you'd just won the Open. You'd never gag over a three-footer. You'd grind your opponents into the dirt.

The best swing thought I ever heard of was that of an unflappable old touring pro. "I just try to hear a dial tone," he said. That's what life sounds like to a dog. Somebody out there is trying to get through with bad news, but the receiver is dangling from the end of its cord. You think of nothing, except maybe dinner and the stuff you've got buried in the yard. You wag your tail a couple of times. And then you swing.

Golf vs. Tennis

JACK NICKLAUS once called tennis a "better" sport than golf—by which he could have meant only that tennis provides more exercise, a point both obvious and irrelevant. In every other way, tennis is inferior. No nassaus! Even dumber shoes! Fuzzy balls! Absurdly uncomplicated rules!

I myself play tennis every so often, at times when Scrabble and shuffleboard are unavailable. It's not a bad way to work up a sweat, I'll admit, but the game has no depth. Tennis is to golf as checkers is to chess. Tennis players don't suddenly wake their families at three in the morning by shouting triumphantly, "I just need to turn my left hand one knuckle to the right!" Tennis players don't go to Penney's to try on pants they don't need, so they can check their swing in the mirrors in the dressing rooms. Tennis players don't sleep in parking lots on Saturday nights.

The reason, of course, is that tennis players don't actually need to play tennis; the game just doesn't inspire that level of commitment. A couple of months ago, at high noon on the hottest Saturday of the summer—a day when the road was scarcely visible through the waves of heat shimmering above it, and the asphalt was the consistency of fresh glazing compound—I drove past the tennis club on my way to the golf course. The courts were empty, because the tennis players had all gone inside to escape the weather. The golf course, needless to say, was full. In fact, I had to wait half an hour to tee off.

You've never heard of a tennis player being struck by lightning, have you?

There is only one moment in tennis when that game comes within shouting distance of golf. That moment occurs when your opponent, having been driven to the baseline by the fury of your return, takes a lunging, desperate swipe at the ball and catches just enough of it to lob it fifty feet into the air, a marshmallow, and the ball is spinning so slowly that you can see the seams on its cover, and it floats high above the net and drifts gently toward the farthest corner of your end of the court, and you instantaneously calculate its trajectory and drop back into the perfect position to smack it to oblivion, and all your options spread out before you, and you can see your opponent shuffling nervously at the edge of your field of vision, and you know exactly what you want to do, and you set your feet and take your racket back slowly, and the ball drops perfectly into the circumference of your swing—teed up, as it were—and you dump it into the net.

A golf moment. The only one in tennis. I rest my case.

Golf Without a Hole

Mᴜ ᴘᴀʀᴇɴᴛꜱ-ɪɴ-ʟᴀᴡ recently sent me a souvenir from
New Zealand, where they were traveling. The souvenir
was two football-shaped golf balls in a fake-velvet bag. At first,
I assumed I was supposed to eat the balls. (My parents-in-law
give me golf-themed edible novelties fairly often, because of
my love for the game.) Just as I was about to throw them away,
though, I realized that the balls, though weirdly shaped, could
be hit with a golf club. So I hit them. They flew dead straight,
end over end, like kicked footballs.

The balls, it turns out, are part of a game called GolfCross,
which was invented in New Zealand and is a variant of regular
golf. I fired off an e-mail seeking more information. About
five seconds later, my telephone rang, and I spent the next half
hour listening to Burton Silver, the game's creator and, possibly, the most enthusiastic person in the southern hemisphere.
The gist of his remarks (slowed down to aid comprehension):
In GolfCross, the target is not a hole but a large net sus-
pended above the ground; an oval ball is more stable in flight
than a round ball is, and it's easier to control; you get to tee up

every shot (on a tee that looks like a rubber thimble on a stick); teeing the ball straight up makes it go straight; leaning the ball to the left makes it go left; placing the ball on the ground in a certain way makes it curve to the right in the air, then bounce to the left when it lands—a shot called "the snake"; GolfCross courses are easy to set up, and New Zealand has four of them.

Silver sent me thirty balls and tees, and I took them to my club on Sunday. After my friends and I had finished our regular match, we played two holes of GolfCross (as a fourteen-some). We didn't have nets, so we used greenside bunkers as our targets. We discovered that the balls don't fly as far as regular balls do, but that they don't slice unless you want them to slice, and that you can make them do tricks Phil Mickelson only dreams of. The medalist (and, therefore, the reigning GolfCross champion of the United States) was my friend Hacker, who played the two holes in a total of four strokes.

All my friends liked GolfCross, so we added Burton Silver's invention to the official playoff rota of our Sunday morning group. You can find out more at his Web site (www.golfcross.com). Think twice before giving him your phone number, though.

The Meg Mallon
Conundrum

OF ALL THE SOCIETAL ILLS for which men are routinely blamed—among them war, crime, famine, and outbreaks of mayhem at the post office—there's one that I've decided to stop feeling guilty about: the relatively lowly status of the women's professional golf tour.

The difference in fortunes between the PGA Tour and the LPGA Tour is certainly stark. By my rough reckoning, the top twenty-five male touring pros earned more money playing golf last year than did the entire female population of the earth, even if you throw in ladies'-day golf shop credits and don't count men's endorsement money.

I'm not saying the difference isn't big; I'm just saying it isn't my fault. In fact, I think the well-known troubles of the LPGA Tour have more to do with women than with men.

The reason I don't feel guilty is that I am a reasonably staunch supporter of the LPGA Tour. I like watching players who, with a hundred and seventy yards left to the flag, are more likely to hit a seven-wood than a seven-iron. I like to mull what I think of as the Meg Mallon Conundrum, which is the disturbing fact that Meg Mallon doesn't hit her driver any farther than I hit mine yet still manages to shoot in the sixties, win big tournaments, and be talked about as one of the best players in the world. I like believing that the swing Tammie Green used in the late stages of her most recent pregnancy will someday lead to a permanent golf cure for middle-aged guys who keep outgrowing their belts. And I like the fact that during LPGA events there is almost no chance that one of the players will suddenly light a cigar.

I know other people who feel the same way I do about the LPGA Tour—and almost all of them are male. In fact, I would bet that at my club there are a lot more men than women who know that Dana Dormann was Dana Lofland before she got married and that Dottie Pepper was Dottie Mochrie before she got divorced. The men know because they watch LPGA tournaments on television and read about its stars in magazines; the women don't because they don't.

That isn't necessarily a terrible thing. If most women consumed televised sports with the same idiotic intensity that most men do, civilization would come to an end. But it may help to explain why the LPGA Tour never quite seems to hit its stride: women's golf will never be a success until women make it one.

Golf on the Shelf

Many of golf's best moments occur off the course. There are the beers on the patio when your round is over. There is the midnight inspiration that sends you tiptoeing into the backyard in your pajamas with a pitching wedge and a sleeve of balls. There are the equipment catalogues that make you feel like a kid with an inside track to Santa Claus. There is that first glimpse of Amen Corner on TV each April—official proof that winter is gone. And there is the pile of golf books and magazines that teeters next to your chair, ready to return you to your favorite frame of mind whenever it's too cold, too dark, or too wet to play.

For most of us, golf improves in retrospect. That triple-bogey on seventeen reveals itself, upon reflection, to have been a double-bogey derailed by an unrepaired ball mark. And if your playing partner hadn't coughed at the top of your backswing on the tee, your drive most likely would have stayed to the left of the water: bogey. And if somebody's dog hadn't dug up that greenside bunker during the night, your sand shot surely would have landed on grass instead of sand,

and you'd have had your par. In fact, you once sank a birdie putt from almost as far away. You can still remember every inch of that curling forty-footer, which broke left instead of right but, because you pushed it, still tumbled in. And today, but for a handful of flukes, you damn near made birdie again.

Reading about golf provides similar opportunities for genial self-deception. The kinks in your game recede as you imagine the clashes of titans. As always, your enjoyment is heightened by the certainty that if *you* had come to the final nine with a lead that big, you wouldn't have let victory slip through your fingers, unlike Palmer. Then a remark of Hogan's reminds you of a grip change your pro recommended last year—a grip change that felt peculiar the one time you tried it, but that might be your ticket (you now see clearly) to the Senior Tour. Then a description of the sixteenth at Cypress Point transports you to the part of your mind where your children are grown, your spouse is merciful, and you have all the money in the world.

On the page, golf is a game you could almost get the hang of. As you read, your slice becomes a gentle draw, and your best shots swell in your memory until they have pushed aside every lip-out, chili dip, pop-up, and shank. Sometimes when I've been reading about golf, a feeling starts to build that's like a smoker's yearning for a cigarette. It's a physical longing, which, as often as not, leads to anxious glances at the clock. Could I get to the driving range and back before the plumber arrives? Will my editor really care if that article is another day late? Isn't there maybe just enough daylight left for a quick nine holes, if I don't bother to change my shoes?

Best of all, reading about golf is less susceptible than golf itself to the depredations of age. When the yips have stolen our putting strokes, when we can no longer lift our drivers, when even a golf cart seems like too much effort, we will still have golf's huge and continually growing library to keep us in the game—even if we have to hire a caddie to read it to us.

Transition

THERE IS A POINT of no return in a golfer's life, and an older friend recently passed it. I know he did, because I saw the evidence in his bag. It was right between his three-wood and his umbrella.

It was a ball retriever.

My friend used to play pretty well. He never won our club championship, but in his prime he was one of the guys a champion had to beat. In a nassau, you wanted him for a partner. In a scramble, you wanted him on your team. He would go for the green in two on a par-five, and he would sink a putt that mattered. He was, locally, a player.

Two or three years ago, his game began to wilt. His draw faded. His fade sliced. He stopped signing up for tournaments. The putts that he gave (and therefore showed that he yearned to be given) crept into the leather, then crept beyond it. Little by little, his focus as a golfer shifted from the hole to the pond.

Golfers who carry ball retrievers are gatherers, not hunters. They've given up the chase. They've climbed as far up the hill as they can climb, and now the paths lead only down. They've stopped tinkering with their grips. They don't practice in the sand. Their dreams are no longer of conquest, but only of salvage.

Golfers who carry ball retrievers don't walk down the center of the fairway anymore. They go the long way, through the tall grass, because that's where the lost drives hide. They stir the weeds with nine-irons as they pass. When they step on something round, they freeze. Instead of searching the tree-tops for a change in the wind, the way they used to, they let their eyes drift lower: there are balls in the woods. If no one is pressing them from behind, they leave their bags and walk along the creek. By the end of the morning, their pockets are bulging. They will never buy another sleeve.

I know a man who bought his ball retriever years ago. He still plays a little, but he's just as happy not to. On Friday afternoons, I see him in the marsh to the right of the first fairway. There's a shallow, silt-choked pond back there. My friend wears rubber boots that come up to his knees. Most of the balls he finds are dark and heavy, but he doesn't throw many back.

His hoard of balls, which he keeps in the trunk of his car, will surely outlast him. But he doesn't think about that. Suddenly, he glimpses something pale in a spot too deep for wading. He extends his ball retriever and threads it through the cattails. He braces his boots in the muck and reaches as far as he dares into the darkness at the bottom of the pond.

The Superintendent's Cup

THE MOST POPULAR TOURNAMENT at my club is the last big one of the season. It's called the Superintendent's Cup, and it's contested by two teams of members. The prize is a silver trophy that was donated by Bob, our superintendent. He and Fran, our pro, serve as non-playing team leaders, and they choose sides from the list of those who sign up. Their selections are the result of lengthy, secretive, beer-assisted negotiations. The tournament is held during four days on consecutive weekends in the fall. Each round has a different format: alternate shot, scramble, best ball, and head-to-head singles. Points accumulate over all four days, and the names of all the players on each year's victorious team are engraved on the base of the cup.

The most unusual feature of the Superintendent's Cup, as weekend club tournaments go, is that it isn't limited to men; nor are the women segregated in a separate flight. Players are placed on the roster where their handicaps fall, with the result that many of the matches—all of which are played at scratch—are co-ed. For more than a few participants in the first Superintendent's Cup, losing to women and defeating men were brand-new experiences. In the years since then, a number of our other tournaments have become co-ed, too. (In our first match in the annual Member-Member a few years ago, my partner, Ray, and I played Evelyn and Carol, to whom we owed a total of fifty-eight strokes over eighteen holes. Ray and I took some ribbing in the clubhouse beforehand, but the match was among the tensest I have ever played, and Ray and I had to birdie two of the last three holes in order to win; even then, the outcome was decided by the final putt. If our opponents had had more match-play experience, they'd have closed us out two holes before.)

Early finishers in the Superintendent's Cup seldom go home when their rounds are over. They head back onto the course to root for their teammates, or they gather on the slope behind the last green. A few years ago, my friend Art had the idea of clearing the thorny brush and poison ivy from that slope, to make more room for spectators. Art did the work himself. Then Bob sank two posts into the ground and bolted a long bench between them. During the Superintendent's Cup, we increase the seating capacity by carrying down chairs from the clubhouse patio. Fran and Bob sit there all day, drinking cognac, smoking cigars, offering encouragement, and updating the scoreboard. On the final Sunday, Bob's assistant, Danny, roasts a pig in a huge barrel-shaped charcoal oven in the parking lot behind the practice green, and Danny's children, who are little, run around. When you finish your match, you fill a paper plate with chunks of pork, grab a beer from the cooler, and head back to the spectator section.

Each team has a color—Fran's is red, and Bob's is blue—and we dress accordingly. A few years ago, Bob chose me to be the captain of his team, and I dressed entirely in blue, including socks and underwear. What sort of captain was I? Well, the competition was so close that if the four matches in which I competed had been thrown out, my team would have won.

On the first day of the first Superintendent's Cup, five or six years ago, the red team accumulated what appeared to be an insurmountable lead, winning seventeen and a half points out of a possible twenty. The results made everybody gloomy—especially the team leaders, who had tried hard to create evenly matched sides. On the final Sunday, though, with sixty points at stake in twenty singles matches, Bob's players somehow managed to overwhelm their opponents, and the impossible occurred. On the last hole of the last match, a gray-haired septuagenarian widow named Pat sank a six-foot putt that tied the entire tournament. No one told her how important her putt was until her ball had dropped—a good thing, Pat said later.

For the playoff, each team's playing captain chose a partner, and those two pairs replayed the eighteenth hole, alternate shot. I don't recall which team won the playoff—and I'm no longer certain which team I was on—but I still remember the roar of the crowd. A photograph of the final scoreboard, showing the two teams tied at sixty points apiece, hangs on a wall in the main room of our clubhouse.

Tiger's Streak:
How We Did It

TIGER WOODS'S STRING of six consecutive PGA Tour victories—which began at the Firestone Country Club in late 1999 and ended at the Pebble Beach Golf Links in early 2000—was a major triumph for my son and me. It ranked right up there with the Chicago Bulls' 1999 NBA Championship, for which, to be perfectly honest, I deserve less credit than my son. (It was he who enabled Michael Jordan to sink the winning basket, by deciding which of our two dogs to squeeze with his left arm while standing on a chair during the game's final seconds.)

Influencing the outcome of televised sporting events is harder than many people believe, because a technique that induces victory today may have the opposite effect tomorrow. Mumbling obscenities, swaying hypnotically, and making hula-like hand motions in front of the screen will usually keep a long putt from going in—especially if the camera never leaves the hole, and the putter is Colin Montgomerie—but this method sometimes fails disastrously, perhaps by accidentally nudging an errant ball onto the correct line. Similarly, my son's most reliable trick, that of drinking water steadily throughout an important contest but not going to the bathroom until it's over, seems to backfire on isolated occasions. Why?

Curiously, the best method for salvaging victory when things are going poorly is usually to turn off the TV—a tactic whose effectiveness may be explained by quantum mechanics: Unless directly observed, athletic competitions, like muons and mesons, exist in all possible states simultaneously, perhaps. Turning off the TV during a big tournament restores the universe's indifference to the final score, thereby giving Tiger (let's say) a chance to rediscover his swing. This quantum effect may also explain why viewers are able to influence even videotaped sporting events—as long as the viewers don't know in advance how everything came out.

What happened at the Buick Invitational, where Tiger tragically ended his streak, by finishing second to Phil Mickelson? I'm sorry to confess that during several of Tiger's must-make putts in the final round, my son and I each kept one hand on Philip Wilkinson's *Illustrated Dictionary of Religions*, which my wife (who teaches Sunday school) had left on a table in front of the TV. The book—whose cover includes a painting of Lakshmi, the Hindu goddess of wealth and good fortune— seemed foolproof. But my son and I, fatally, overlooked two crucial details: the book's author's name is eerily similar to Phil Mickelson's, and my wife doesn't know anything about golf.

Between Clubs

Dꜱ URING A GOLF TRIP to Ireland a few years ago, I played a round at Lahinch with a young woman whose handicap was two. "And she plays to it," the pro warned me as we set out. She was a college student, and she had grown up in a modest house just across the road from the club. The faces of her irons looked like Ben Hogan's, with dark, nickel-sized abrasions over the sweet spots. The irons were so worn that I assumed they must have been handed down to her from some previous generation, but she said that she had bought them, new, just two years before. "I like to practice," she explained.

On one hole, after she had creamed a drive past mine down the center of the fairway, I asked her how far she hit her seven-iron. She looked thoughtful for a moment, frowned, and said, "I don't really know." When I laughed, she said she seldom thought in terms of yardage, because on an Irish seaside course there were so many other factors to consider: the strength and direction of the wind, the firmness of the ground, the shape of the green, the shape of the shot, the season. She played a seven-iron when the shot looked to her like a seven-iron shot; beyond that, she didn't know. Obviously, her intuition had been informed by years of experience and careful, if unconscious, observation. But raw measurement played no part.

You may think this story has no bearing on those of us who don't wear holes through the sweet spots of our golf clubs. But I've begun to think it may. While playing a few months later on an unfamiliar course, I drove my ball into an awkward spot, far from any yardage marker. I didn't want to hold up my friends by tramping back to the fairway and attempting to triangulate the distance, so I studied the pin for a moment and decided that it seemed to be about a seven-iron away. I swung. My ball soared high above the green and landed within a respectable distance of the cup. If you had asked me then how far I had hit my shot, I would have looked thoughtful for a moment, frowned, and said, "I don't really know."

It wasn't that I had suddenly developed "feel." It was just that, for the first time during the round, I had hit a shot while believing that the club in my hand was the right one, not the wrong one. Most of us are so approximate with our irons that knowing the exact yardage creates more problems than it solves. A 138-yard shot might seem to call for, say, an eight-iron. But you just topped a six-iron about that distance, and you sometimes hit a nine-iron longer. Still, the flag looks farther away—a lot farther than 138. But your seven-iron goes 150, so how could a seven be right? Focusing on yardage in a situation like that creates doubt, not confidence. And doubt is the death of a fragile swing.

The trick would be somehow to play every course the way you play your course at home. There's a par-three at my regular club whose length I don't even know—I just know what I hit there. When the hole looks longer, as it sometimes does, I swing a little harder; when it looks shorter, I drop back a club. Knowing the yardage at this point would only confuse me. Knowledge, in golf, is seldom as useful as conviction.

Dealing with the Devil

I F YOU COULD TRADE I.Q. for driving distance, would you do it? Three hundred yards up the middle every time, and all you'd have to sacrifice would be hardcover books and your subscription to the ballet. It might not feel like much of a loss. The world is full of people who are too smart for their own good, but you never hear anyone complaining about being too long and straight off the tee. Your spouse might even find the new you more appealing, since you'd have trouble thinking of impudent remarks. And to your regular foursome you'd be a god.

Or what if steroids would cut your handicap by ten strokes—or twenty? There would be side effects to consider. ("Moon face" and "buffalo hump" are among the more colorful-sounding ones, not to mention heart disease, liver damage, and disappearing testicles.) But if steroids would give you a crack at the Senior Tour, or even just the club championship, would you be tempted? I hate what drugs have done to sports, but when I think of how I might react if birdies came in a bottle—well, I feel less sanctimonious.

It's probably lucky that Faustian bargains are hard to come by. A friend of mine in college once rolled a blank sheet of paper into his typewriter, turned out the lights, and offered his soul to the devil for a five-page, double-spaced essay on *The Merchant of Venice*. When he turned the lights back on, an hour later, the paper was still blank. For that and other reasons, he needed an extra year to earn his degree. But he did earn it, and he now has a good job, a nice house, and a happy family. If that Shakespeare essay really had materialized, his life almost certainly would have followed a different path.

The conventional route to self-improvement seldom seems compelling, however. It's hard to get excited about taking lessons and practicing chip shots. How much easier it seems to pin your hopes on the devil, or a three-thousand-dollar set of irons.

For that matter, I wonder whether most of us truly want to improve. We all say we want to play better, but we don't always act as though we do. Most of the golfers I know, including myself, have chronic swing problems that could be solved with professional help—yet we never face them squarely. I sometimes play with a guy whose club of choice for bunker shots is a rake. When his ball goes into the sand, he scrapes it out and heads to the next tee. "I'm in my pocket," he mutters. A lesson or two would patch him up, but in twenty-five years of playing he has never taken one. Why?

The answer may be that struggling golfers are like dysfunctional families. My friend is afraid to deal with his bunker trouble because at some level he's worried that treating it would turn up dozens of worse problems, leading to years of discouraging therapy. Like most of us, he'd rather stumble along in deep denial, treating triple-bogeys as a fact of life, dreaming of a magic pill.

Nomenclature

A MINOR MOVEMENT is underway in the golf world. The movement is confined, for the moment, to television broadcast booths, but it may spread someday to the general population. The aim of the movement is to rename fairway woods.

Woods, as you have surely noticed, are no longer made of wood. My first driver—which was partly responsible for my decision, at the age of thirteen, to give up golf for twenty-five years—was a two-generation hand-me-down with a persimmon head that could have spent its winters as the foot of a Queen Anne chair. Nowadays, in contrast, even seven-year-olds demand titanium. I know three or four players who still carry woods made of wood, but they are all over seventy, and each of them is stubborn, cheap, ignorant, or a combination of the three. You seldom see wooden clubs anymore even in the golf bags of estranged wives, who occupy the lowest rung on the club recycling ladder.

The question, though, is whether this change in technology necessitates a change in terminology. Various prominent television commentators have decided that it does. They refer to woods now as "metals," saying, for example, that a certain player has elected to go for the green with a "fairway metal" of some kind—perhaps a "three-metal." On CBS recently, Jim Nantz referred to a fairway wood generically as "a metal-headed club."

There are three things wrong with this trend. The first is that it creates more confusion than it eliminates, since all modern golf clubs, including irons and putters, are "metal-headed." The second is that "wood" is no more anachronistic than "iron." (Irons haven't been made of iron since Britain was ruled by Romans. Should we start calling those clubs "alloys"?) The third is that eschewing "wood" is excessively fastidious, like objecting to the use of the (useful) word "hopefully." The television commentators are proposing a solution for a problem that doesn't exist.

Besides, retaining an archaic expression creates the possibility for creative revisionism later on.

"Why are woods called 'woods'?" your great-great-granddaughter may ask you someday.

"Well, Little One," you can explain, "there was an awfully good player back around the turn of the century. He hit the ball farther than anybody else, and he won every prize there was to win. In fact, I taught him everything he knew. Woods were named after him."

The Old-Guy Game

I WENT ALONE to a golf course in a neighboring town the other day. There were four carts parked beside the first tee, and a young guy in a Greg Norman hat was taking gigantic practice swings in preparation for slicing his drive into the eighteenth fairway. The assistant pro offered to run me out to the second tee so I could jump ahead, and I accepted. A group on the third hole waved me through. I ran into another group on five, so I ducked behind the snack shack and went to seven. I had clear sailing for one shot. That caught me up to a threesome of old-timers, who were moving down the fairway as slowly as if they were worried about land mines. They invited me to play through—many clear holes lay ahead—but I asked if I could join them instead.

I like playing with old guys. My tempo drops out of the red zone, and I stop trying to hit the ball farther than I can—the opposite of what happens when I play with college students. I enjoy hearing stories about what the course or the club or the members were like forty years ago, when everything was better than it is now. Every so often, an old guy who can no longer reach the fairway with a driver will turn out to be a former hotshot—as I'll discover later, when I recognize his name on one of the plaques on the clubhouse walls.

I like looking into old guys' bags: mismatched irons, woods made of wood, grips resurfaced with electrical tape, chippers, Gintys, Samurais, 23-woods, putters with punch marks on their faces, and ball retrievers that extend so far you could rescue your glasses from the Marianas trench. The guy in the Greg Norman hat would sneer, but to me those golf bags prove that with good luck and the right equipment you can keep playing until the day you drop.

You also need the right swing, of course. Two of my three elderly companions the other day had one that I've been studying: a short, turn-less lunge—the same move you make when you throw dirt with a shovel. It's the old-guy swing, and it's the product of a compromise worked out by old bones, stiff muscles, and osteoarthritis. I've been studying it lately because I suspect that someday it will be my swing, and I want to be prepared.

Both players aimed left and hit right. They took their clubs back belt-high, then leaned forward and swatted. Their shots didn't go very far, but we never had to look for a ball, except mine. After three three-woods apiece, they were close enough to the green to hit pitching wedge, just about the only iron that either of them still bothered with. They drilled their putts, got two strokes, and took the hole with net birdies, while I three-putted for a five.

I still nurse a fantasy that I will wake up one morning and be Ernie Els, or even Morris Hatalsky. But it pays to be realistic, and time is running out. There's a lot to be said for the old-guy game. If my regular foursome wouldn't make fun of me, I'd almost be tempted to switch right now.

Lies

A LAWYER FRIEND OF MINE spent a couple of years as a public defender. He was surprised to discover that the nation's jails are filled with innocent victims. "I didn't do it," his clients invariably protested. A guy could have been caught with a gun in his hand, blood on his shoes, and a body in the trunk of his car, yet he would greet with incredulity any suggestion that he might have something to explain.

Great competitive golfers have the same attitude. Picture Seve Ballesteros in his prime. He has a twenty-foot putt for birdie, and he rolls his ball a quarter-inch wide. His jaw drops, his eyebrows bristle, and he turns to the gallery in outraged disbelief. Who planted this grass? Is my ball defective? Did somebody lift the edge of the green?

The great players don't take their misses personally. At the peak of his game, Seve treated his bad shots as impartially as if they had been struck by his partner in a Scotch foursome. He was open to all explanations, except any that could be framed in the first person. Missing putts was not something that he did; it was something that was done to him—by a spike mark, by a noisy camera, by a green that obstinately declined to tilt in the direction he had read. A slice into the woods was no different from a bad hop off a sprinkler head. It was just the rub of the green.

Nick Faldo, playing in the final pair in the final round of the British Open in 1996, pushed a drive many yards to the right of the fairway on one of the closing holes, then hit a poor approach that never came near the green. His reaction? An angry oath about the "ground." Two bad shots in a row, and the only culprit he could think of was the earth itself. His chance of winning now diminished, he blamed the planet.

Those of us who don't win major championships tend to have a different point of view. It's our good shots, not our bad ones, that we view as inexplicable. My birdies to me seem like lucky accidents, while my triple bogeys are windows on my soul. If I hit three or four good drives in a row, a horrible tension begins to build. Where did *this* swing come from? When the hurried slash returns, I'm almost relieved.

When a great player admits to playing poorly, his confession has a ring of insincerity. "I didn't putt well today" is not an acknowledgment of failure. It's a neutral observation about a phenomenon as impersonal as the weather. A great player views a swing flaw as just that, a flaw in a swing, not a deficiency in himself.

Hauled in chains before a judge, I wouldn't make a convincing liar. "Yes, I did it," I'd sob, "and it's even worse than you think." Nicklaus in his heyday wouldn't have cracked like that. So what if my fingerprints are on the gun? I never even met that guy. What state did you say this happened in? Somebody must be trying to frame me.

Boss

My friend Hacker has invented a new game, which he calls Boss. He and I played it with our friend Ray during a one-day road trip to another town not long ago, and it's a good one. It's a supplemental game—something you play in addition to your nassau, your skins game, your double-digit-handicap championship of the world, or whatever you've got going. It shares the single most important feature of all truly worthwhile golf games: astonishing complexity. Here's how it works.

Each player arrives at the first tee with a stake of eighteen one-dollar bills. The players in the group then establish a playing order—one through four in a foursome—by drawing straws, calling coin tosses, throwing balls, chipping toward a tee marker, throwing tees, or pulling numbers out of a hat.

The first player in the order becomes the Boss for the first hole. In our match, that was me. As the Boss, I got to announce a rule that we all had to follow on that hole, at the risk of losing one or more of our eighteen dollar bills. My rule: anyone who drives into a fairway bunker owes a buck to anyone who doesn't. No one did, so our money stayed in our pockets, and Ray (No. 2) took over as the Boss on the second tee.

The key to winning money in Boss is to create rules that reward your own strengths, penalize your opponents' weaknesses, or (ideally) both. Ray's rule for the second hole—anyone who reaches the green in (net) regulation wins a dollar from anyone who doesn't—took advantage of the fact that he hits the ball farther and straighter than Bob or I do. Bob and I didn't reach in regulation, so we each had to pay a buck to Ray, who did.

Bob, the No. 3 player, was the next in line to be the Boss, but, because he had lost money on the previous hole, he had to skip his turn. I had lost money, too, so I was passed over as well—meaning that Ray got to be the Boss again. If you choose your rules craftily and play reasonably well, you can sometimes call the shots for several holes in a row. (No rule can be repeated, though; the longest driver in the group can't simply keep saying, "Longest drive gets paid.")

We were also playing Escrow Skins (see page 24) that day, in addition to Boss, and the two games were satisfyingly complementary. On a long par-five where I needed to make a par in order to secure four skins that I had in escrow, for example, Bob, as the Boss, ruled that anyone who was left of the fairway off the tee would owe a dollar to anyone who wasn't. On that particular hole, the fairway was narrow and the right rough was death, and Bob was trying to make me think twice about purposely driving into the light rough on the left—the most sensible shot for someone who needed to make a safe par. (I managed to hit the fairway but ended up making bogey anyway—a long story.)

We came up with some other interesting rules that day: three-putt pays; first ball in gets paid; shortest drive in the fairway gets paid (on a hole where the longest drive had the best chance of winning a skin); closest to the hole off the tee (on a par-three) gets paid; anyone in any hazard pays a buck for every hazard he hits (on a hole with water left of the fairway, right of the fairway, and in front of the green). A few weeks later, my friend Gene, who doesn't hit the ball very far, came up with my favorite Boss rule of all time: "Anybody who drives past me owes me a buck."

Once you've lost all eighteen of your dollars, you're finished, unless you elect to re-liquefy and go on. Naturally, the first round of beers afterward is paid for by the day's big winner.

Drive for Dough

"DRIVE FOR SHOW, PUTT FOR DOUGH" is among the oldest truisms in professional golf. But crude statistical analysis proves the underlying thesis to be questionable at best. The longest drivers on tour routinely out-earn the guys who take the fewest putts. And forget about accuracy: four of the tour's ten longest drivers earned spots on the U.S. Ryder Cup team for 2002, while just one of the ten straightest did.

Drive for dough, putt for stats.

Well, that's an exaggeration, too. Quite obviously, lousy putters don't last long on any golf course. Even more to the point, true putting skill is impossible to assess numerically. In 2001, Tiger Woods ranked a hundred and second in "putting average" and a hundred and thirty-fourth in "putts per round," the two measures used by the tour to quantify putting success. Yet does anyone really think that Craig Kanada, who placed sixth in the first category and first in the second, putted better than Tiger Woods? Kanada played in twenty-eight tournaments in 2001, won a bit more than a hundred and thirty thousand dollars, and failed to keep his card for 2002, while Woods—well, you know what Woods did. If I had to pick one guy in the world to sink a curling forty-footer to save my life, it wouldn't be the guy who ranked first on tour in "total putting."

Statistics aside, raw animal power deserves more respect, as an on-course strategy, than it usually receives. If your opponents are forty yards longer off the tee than you are, they are probably also ten or fifteen yards longer with every iron. That means they'll be hitting wedges to greens you'd be lucky to reach with long irons. Even if erratic tee shots force those big knockers to play from screwy positions much of the time, their approaches are going to be easier than yours. A demoralized Colin Montgomerie, after being demoted by Tiger Woods to the B flight at the 1997 Masters, said, "The greatest asset in golf, I believe, is length."

Distance is even more important for you and me than it is for the pros, because in our case a lack of power is usually a symptom of a more fundamental problem: a crummy swing. We are short not because we have shrewdly traded distance for precision but because we lash at the ball, come over the top, strangle the club, or succumb to any of a thousand other catastrophic swing flaws. For players like us, distance and accuracy are the two sides of a single coin. Getting longer—by learning to swing correctly—would also make us straighter.

Alone at Last

MY BROTHER'S FATHER-IN-LAW received three D's and a C-minus one semester in college, and the dean demanded an explanation. "Well, you know what happens," my brother's father-in-law said, "when you put all your effort into one course."

I feel that way about my short game at the moment. There was a brief period, a few months ago, when I could get up and down from anywhere. But my touch has vanished, and my putter and wedges feel strange in my hands, like golf clubs in a dream. Every ball either stops short or rolls long. The cup looks scarcely large enough to hold the flagstick. No matter how much effort I put into my chipping and putting, I can't get back to where I was.

Or maybe practicing is the problem. On the putting green, my mind wanders after a dozen strokes. At the range, I hit too many shots too fast, and I quickly push my tempo up to the tennis end of the spectrum. My rhythm would be fine for volleys at the net, but it's all wrong for soft lobs over sand. And working only makes it worse.

What I really need to do is play a few rounds alone. My yips don't yip when no one is watching. My putts don't leak below the hole. In fact, my whole game works better. My arms are ribbons and my head keeps still. I stay behind. I don't come over. By the time the clubhouse comes back into view, I'm pretty sure I'll never make another bogey. I could beat all the guys who beat me now if I could play them *in absentia*.

Solo golf is so easy that you shouldn't have to turn in your scores. It gives you a glimpse of the golfer you might have been and might still be—a player who goes for it in two, slams three-footers against the back of the cup, and always reaches for the driver. When you play alone, your inner self sits down and lets your better self play through. By the time you finish, your swing is back where it's supposed to be. You can face the world again.

The rule book is unkind to those of us who like to play by ourselves. A single golfer "has no standing and should give way to a match of any kind," the U.S.G.A. says. That means that if you're stuck between two slow foursomes, the group ahead doesn't have to acknowledge your existence and the group behind can require you to let them through.

Consequently, the best time to play alone is when the course is alone as well—say, late one afternoon toward the end of the season. The parking lot is almost empty. The pro has gone home. You don't feel tight, so there's no need to bend or stretch or even take a practice swing. After teeing off, you can grab your bag while your ball is still in the air. You know where your drive is going to be.

The Fundamentals of Glof

I HAD A GLIMPSE of my soul not long ago. Like most people accorded that opportunity, I didn't like what I saw.

The occasion was a thirty-six-hole stroke-play tournament in a neighboring city. Stroke play (also known as medal play) is what the pros play on tour. It is different from match play, the hole-by-hole competition that is the basis of virtually every game you and I play, from Sunday-morning nassaus to the finals of the club championship. In match play, every hole is its own contest, and a golfer can always stem a burgeoning disaster by hollering "I'm in my pocket!" and heading to the next tee.

In a stroke-play tournament, in contrast, your pocket isn't a part of the course. Every shot counts, and your round isn't over until your ball has touched the bottom of eighteen cups. Your opponent can't knock away the two-footer you are dreading, and you can't scoop up your own ball in disgust after rolling a three-foot bogey putt four feet past the hole. A friend of mine once drove three balls out of bounds on a difficult par-five in a regional amateur tournament, then *purposely* played his fourth ball (and seventh stroke) into a lateral hazard on the opposite side of the fairway—just so he could leave the tee. In match play, he could have conceded the hole after the second banana, no worse off than if he'd made a birdie to his opponent's eagle.

In stroke play, your bad shots don't come back to haunt you. They haunt you right now. And every mistake makes the next swing harder.

My horrifying self-revelation was similar to that of a friend, who arrived at the first tee one morning looking dangerously depressed.

"What's the matter?" I asked. "Lose your job?"

"No, worse," he said. "I saw a videotape of my swing." He sniffed back tears. "All these years," he went on, "I assumed that my swing looked like the swings on TV. It *felt* like the swings on TV. But now I've actually seen myself. I look like a marionette chopping wood."

On the Internet once, I stumbled across a news-group debate concerning the difference between amateurs and pros. The consensus of the participants (all of whom were weekend golfers) was that the pros have it awfully easy: free equipment, good caddies, immaculate courses, accurate yardage, plenty of practice. If the rest of us had the same advantages, the weekend golfers argued, our handicaps would plummet.

After playing two rounds of crummy golf in a meaningless amateur tournament with my heart pounding at the top of my esophagus, I can tell you for a fact that those Internet golfers were wrong. The game that you and I play on weekends is so different from the game the pros play that it ought to have a different name. How about *glof*?

Most of us glofers have a wildly inflated sense of how good we are—even if we think we stink. Eight-handicappers, for instance, tend to think of themselves as eight strokes worse than Davis Love. They figure that if they could just trim their U.S.G.A. index down to zero, they could quit their job at the bank and make a living playing on TV. But that's an absurd delusion. A typical eight-handicapper, thrown into the field of a typical tour event, would be lucky to shoot 95, if not 105, while a middling tour pro having a decent day might well shoot 66. So an eight-handicapper's *real* handicap—in relation to the scores of the big boys under tournament conditions in any format where every shot counts—is more like thirty or forty. The same game the pros play? We're lucky they let us use the same balls.

Resting in Peace

M Y GOLF BUDDY Hacker had some trouble with a bunker shot on the final hole of our little course not long ago. As his wedge dug into the sand, he felt a stab of pain in his arm and chest, making him wonder if he had struck a buried stone. He finished the hole, drank a couple of cold ones, took part in a putting contest, went home to finish some chores in his yard, and, a day or two later, made an appointment with his doctor.

As it turned out, he'd had a heart attack. The rest of us watched his recovery with interest, not only because we had been eyeing his new driver—which had given him a minimum of ten extra yards—but also because his misfortune had revived local interest in an old idea of mine. That idea has to do with a small terrace situated between our clubhouse and our practice green. There are a dozen or so chairs on the terrace, including one reserved for our superintendent. When our big Sunday-morning match is over, we all sit in the chairs for an hour or two, drinking beer and eating hamburgers, which we take turns providing. We watch golfers teeing off on

the first hole and putting out on the last; on one golden afternoon a few years ago, we hung around long enough to watch
the sun go down, then ordered some pizzas. The entire terrace measures only about two hundred square feet, but it's one
of my favorite spots on earth.

It was while sitting there one afternoon that I had my big
idea. "Boys," I said, "if anything happens to me, I'd like the
rest of you to get hold of me before my wife does, and bury me
right here, under one of these pavers." The terrace is covered
with rectangular bluestone slabs, which are just the right size
to be engraved with a name, a couple of dates, and a few
important statistics, such as lifetime lowest handicap index
and worst score ever shot in competition. A couple of trees on
our course bear the names of dearly departed members, but
we don't currently do anything with the members themselves.

"I don't know," my friend Bill objected. "Bluestone isn't
much good for engraving. Maybe we ought to use granite."

"Aren't there laws against burying people under patios?"
someone asked.

"I think a golf club is a sovereign entity, like an Indian
reservation."

The discussion continued for an hour or so. Then someone said, "You know, the whole thing wouldn't seem quite so
depressing, if you knew you'd always be here." We nodded.
And we all went home and forgot about it, until Hacker had
his problem on the final hole.

Well, Hacker survived—and thank goodness for that. He

has so much of my best-ball money that I'm going to need at least another two or three decades to win it all back. But I feel at peace with myself, now that I've settled the unsettling question of where to spend eternity. Given a choice, I'd take the slab directly under the fence post that has a bottle opener screwed to it. But just about any of them would do.

Me and My Laser

Bowing to wifely pressure, I swore off golf junk a while back. When golf-related catalogs arrived by mail, I tossed them into the trash without checking to see what was new in the world of anti-slice tees, on-course rain protection for cigars, and tungsten-tipped groove-cleaning utensils. I stopped forcing my kids to spend Sunday afternoons trailing gloomily behind me among the aisles at Nevada Bob's. I quit watching infomercials on the Golf Channel. For a whole week, I didn't buy anything that had anything to do with golf.

Then, one afternoon, I settled down with a hunting-and-fishing catalog, which had arrived in that day's mail. I don't hunt or fish, so I figured that I was safe. Ambassadeur anti-backlash reels. Hastings super-full special-extended turkey-choke tubes. Camouflage denim jeans with generous relaxed-fit sizing. I was interested but unseduced. For a whole half-hour, I happily read with no temptation to buy.

Then it happened. On page 164, I spotted what at first looked like a pair of binoculars but turned to be a laser range finder. A laser range finder! The illustration showed a large deer-type animal caught in some cross hairs. Beneath its feet was the reading "103 yards." I had no trouble imagining a flagstick stuck in the ground on the spot where the deer was standing. My laser range finder arrived the next day by overnight express.

The distance from my back door to the stone wall at the top of my yard is 68 yards. From the top of the kids' tree house to the back of the basketball backstop is 93 yards. From the front step to the middle of the dog (at that particular moment) was 32 yards. When I could find nothing else at home to measure, I headed to the course.

For some time, I'd suspected that the target flags on our driving range were incorrectly marked. Sure enough, the 100-yard flag is just 97 yards from the center of the tee. (Could this explain a recent, baffling up-tick in my handicap?) A friend of mine was practicing with his driver. Measuring surreptitiously, I discovered that his standard 250-yard drive goes (as I had suspected) about 220 yards. When he leaned down to tee up another ball, I bathed his back with laser beams, softening him up for our subsequent match. I thought of a possible feature for future range finders: a readout that would tell you when you aimed the device at people, not only how far away they are, but also how much they make.

After several weeks, I must admit, my range finder no longer seemed quite so interesting. Pretty soon, in fact, I stopped wearing it on my belt during trips to the grocery store. But I'm still glad I own it. (That's the part my wife doesn't understand.) I keep it in the closet where I store most of my other golf junk, and, every once in a while, when I'm having trouble keeping my mind on my work, I pull it out and double-check the distance between my office window and the garage.

Totally in the Dark

THE MAIN PROBLEM WITH NIGHT—the fact that you can't play golf in it—has been solved, as far as I'm concerned. A few years ago, some friends invited me to tee it up at nine o'clock on a moonless August night. Needless to say, we didn't have to wait in line for a tee time. We divided into two scramble teams, consumed a case and a half of beer, managed to keep all the golf carts out of the pond, and played nine holes in a couple of hours. The scores, surprisingly, were roughly what they might have been if the sun had been shining—or maybe they were better. Two down with two to go, my team leveled the match by finishing birdie, eagle.

Playing golf in the dark would be impossible (or at any rate extraordinarily unpleasant) without equipment designed for that purpose. We used Nitelite Golfballs, which glow like nuclear fuel and are sold in golf shops and sporting-goods stores. You light up each one by inserting a slender plastic cartridge filled with luminescent green goo. My son used to like to break open the cartridges, rub the goo on his hands, and chase his sister or our pets around the yard. The balls don't go nearly as far as regular golf balls do, but in the air they look like tracer bullets—a major compensation. They also look cool as they tumble down through the branches of a pine tree, or sink slowly to the bottom of the pond.

The first time I played in the dark, I had trouble getting off the tee. You aren't supposed to look at your golf club as you swing it, of course, but my brain at first rebelled at the sudden invisibility of my driver. Fran, in contrast, says he swings better in the dark: the only issue for him is tempo. But he has a lot more faith in his swing than I have in mine. My friend Jim, who has a twenty-plus handicap and has struggled with his game for years, also swings better in the dark, for some reason. He now talks about buying a golf cap that he can pull down over his eyes.

We tee up all our shots except chips and putts, to reduce damage to the course, because divots are impossible to keep track of in the dark. Lately, we've begun playing with just one club apiece—usually a six-iron or a seven-iron—to eliminate the hassle of lugging around a full arsenal, and to keep a free hand for beer. (Golf carts are also more trouble than they're worth when you can't see where you're going.)

Surprisingly, perhaps, almost everyone I've played night golf with has seemed to putt pretty well. In fact, we all probably putt better at night than we do during the day. Bob, who seldom plays but likes to hang around with us and smoke cigars, aims a flashlight at the cup from directly above it, creating a target perhaps two feet in diameter. Somehow, that small lighted area, in combination with the glow of the golf ball, tells you everything you need to know about distance, slope, and break. With less input to confuse you, you can't over-intellectualize. Your brain doesn't get in the way.

Toward the end of a round of night golf a few years ago, I said, "Boys, it's too bad we'll have to go home when we're finished. Some time, we should stay on the golf course all night—maybe pitch tents by the second green." Everybody laughed. But then we got to thinking. Not long ago, we actually did it.

Our golf-course sleep-over began at five o'clock on a sweltering Saturday evening. We divided into ten two-man better-ball teams and played nine holes of regular golf: ten bucks a head, losers wash the dishes. Then we grilled steaks in the parking lot behind the clubhouse, played Putting for Dollars on the practice green while we waited for the sky to get dark, divided into scramble teams and played nine holes of night golf, played Putting for Dollars with glowing balls, and rolled dice in the clubhouse until we could no longer keep our eyes open. At 4:30 or so, we went to bed. My daughter, who was eighteen at the time, went to a big sleep-over of her own that night, and she told me later that she was impressed my friends had stayed up a full hour later than hers.

The guys I play golf with all snore, so we couldn't use tents. Instead, we slept in our cars, which we spaced at the widest possible intervals around the parking lot. I had customized my family's minivan by removing the rear seats, covering the floor with cushions from the couch on our porch, and covering the cushions with sleeping bags. It was the most comfortable bed I ever slept in.

Shortly after dawn, I was awakened by the smell of frying bacon. Hacker is incapable of sleeping past 5:30—he's a building contractor—so he had started making breakfast. One by one, the other campers stumbled in. We ate scrambled eggs with the bacon and drank coffee, then stumbled back out to wait for the guys whose wives hadn't let them spend the night. Finally, at 7:30, we did what we always do on Sunday mornings: we played golf.

I should mention that we got into a certain amount of trouble. At 2:30 in the morning, someone played a Bruce Springsteen CD at close to full volume on his car stereo, prompting complaints from neighbors, and we left the clubhouse kitchen in approximately the same shape in which my daughter and her friends left the kitchen of the house where they spent the night. We also annoyed some of our club's tennis players, who don't think recreation should be fun. The evening turned out pretty well, though, all things considered. And we all feel a lot closer to our golf course, now that we have spent the night with it.

Atlantic City

ON THE WEEKEND FOLLOWING COLUMBUS DAY, my Sunday-morning golf buddies and I drive to Atlantic City, which is about four hours south of where we live, and conduct a three-day, end-of-season, goodbye-to-golf-until-next-year extravaganza. We take Fran and Bob with us, and we stay in a hotel that has security gates on the inside of the lobby, to protect neighboring merchants from the guests. The hotel's name is similar to that of a famous Atlantic City hotel; the first year we went, several of the guys in our group mistakenly tried to check in there. It was interesting to see the expressions on their faces when they finally arrived at the place where we were really staying. The rooms at our hotel have hard, napless, gummy carpeting, like the stuff you sometimes find in the vicinity of indoor swimming pools. It makes you want to keep your shoes on unless you are in your bed.

The main attraction of our hotel is that it offers cheap golf packages. In fact, playing golf in Atlantic City with my Sunday-morning group costs about the same as staying at home and watching TV. The fee we pay includes not only three rounds of golf at high-quality courses but also pretty good non-self-service buffet breakfasts at our hotel. On Friday night one year, somebody persuaded the hotel's bartender to come back at six the next morning to make us Bloody Marys to go with our free scrambled eggs. At six the next morning, it turned out, hardly anybody actually wanted a Bloody Mary, but we all ordered them anyway, so that the bartender wouldn't feel foolish for having come to work twelve hours before the beginning of his shift. The Bloody Marys didn't taste nearly as bad as anyone had expected, so we ordered some more before leaving for the course, and then, at the course, we ordered some more. The golf-course Bloody Marys, which were poured from plastic jugs that looked almost exactly like divot-mix containers, tasted like something a gastroenterologist might make you drink before x-raying your lower intestine.

The wagering we do on our Atlantic City trip is even more complicated than the wagering we do at home. Before teeing off on Friday afternoon, everybody gives a hundred dollars to Hacker, who stores the money in a leather pouch all weekend and keeps track of our games on charts that he prints in his office before we leave. To fit everything onto the charts, he has to write so small that he needs his reading glasses. One year, just after going to bed on Saturday night, he became worried that he had lost the charts, so he stayed up until dawn attempting to recreate his records from a pile of scorecards, which he had stuffed into the pocket of his golf bag. As the sun was coming up, he suddenly thought of looking in his car, where he found the lost charts lying on the front seat. At lunch that day, when he told me what had happened, I said that in future years he should simply pretend to keep track of our games and then, on Sunday afternoon, give each player back his original hundred dollars, and say, "Here's what you won."

The first year we went to Atlantic City, our trip coincided with the Miss America Pageant, and a few of us took our hotel's shuttle bus into town around midnight to see if anything was going on. We found Miss America–related trash strewn all over the boardwalk, where many overweight people were walking in groups while wearing tee-shirts that proclaimed their support for one contestant or another. The pageant was over by that point, so virtually all of these people were proclaiming their support for contestants who had already gone back to their hotel rooms in tears. A number of lesser beauty pageants had also taken place in Atlantic City that night, and we occasionally saw evidence of those, including a few dozen teenage girls in sashes and ball gowns who had clearly decided that they weren't going to even try to walk gracefully in their high heels anymore. Then we wandered into one of the big casinos and spent about an hour absorbing cigarette smoke with our clothing as we watched other people losing money. Then we went back to our hotel, where half a dozen of us played poker for Tic-Tacs with the hotel's manager while the bartender sang karaoke songs.

Not everybody who goes on our Atlantic City trip is capable of playing poker for Tic-Tacs at two in the morning and then playing thirty-six holes of golf a few hours later, so the second round on Saturday is strictly optional. The first year we went, only eight of us wanted to play, so we teed off as two foursomes. I was in the first foursome. After a few holes, we ran into an extremely slow couple, who were new to golf and, clearly, had never heard of the custom of inviting faster players to play through. To pass the time, we invited the foursome behind us to join us, and played as an eightsome for a while. Even as an eightsome, though, we were still too fast. Then a single player, who was not a part of our group, also caught up to us, and we invited him to join us as well. On one par-five, to alleviate our boredom, all nine of us lined up across the bottom of the fairway and teed off at the same time.

The second year we went to Atlantic City, twelve people wanted to play on Saturday afternoon, so we divided into two six-man scramble teams. The starter wouldn't let us play as six-somes, even though there was nobody else on the course, so we pretended that we were really just four threesomes until we got out of his sight. There wasn't much daylight left, so we didn't play many holes. I don't remember exactly how many holes we did play, and I would be surprised if anybody else does, either, considering how often one or another of us had to drive back down a fairway to pick up a beer can that had fallen, or been thrown, out of a cart. I do know that my sixsome won both the scramble and an unofficial one-hole extra competition, which we added because there was still just enough light to see our hands in front of our faces. We played that extra hole as a twelvesome, and there was some danger that the moon would come out before the last player had teed off.

When we were finished, we held a cart race back to the clubhouse, on a road that Ray had noticed on the other side of a hedge. Getting all the carts through the hedge turned out to be quite a problem, but the road was wide and empty. Ray cheated, by starting well ahead of the signal, so his entry was scratched. I hung off the side of my cart, which Brendan was driving, and tried to undo the strap holding Gene's golf bag onto the back of his cart, while Gene steered evasively.

On the last day of our trip that year, we played a good course at a club that had a decent restaurant with a terrace overlooking one of the holes, and, before we drove home, we ate lunch on the terrace. There was only one waitress covering the bar, the restaurant, and the terrace, and we sat for a very long time before she even brought us menus. She took our orders eventually, but nothing else happened for about half an hour. Finally, Uncle Frank announced that he had worked as a waiter at a resort in the Catskills when he was a young man, and that he was going to help our waitress take care of us. He got water and silverware for all of us, and then he brought us our beers. The chef was surprised when Uncle Frank walked into the kitchen and began loading baskets of bread onto a tray, but Uncle Frank explained what he was doing, and, pretty soon, he and the chef were chatting like old friends. Then Uncle Frank brought us our lunches and refilled our beers. When we were finished, he brought us our checks and told us that we had to leave big tips. As we went out to our cars, the waitress looked at him like she wanted to marry him.

Bonus Days

THE PLACE TO BE when the year's first snow arrives is on a golf course. It's a trick I've managed twice in the past ten years. Both times, the day began without a hint that winter was about to become irrevocable. Both times, the first flakes looked at first like blowing leaves, or bits of ash. Then the clouds let go and the course fell silent, as though a hidden hand somewhere had wound the volume down.

The greens turned white before the fairways did. A putted ball, after rolling a foot, became too fat to turn. On the long walk back to the clubhouse, I dragged my putter along the ground, leaving a dark stripe beside dark footprints. I saw Bob on another fairway, heading out to pull the flags. Putting was over till spring.

I know people who live in places where golf can be played on grass year-round. They gloat when they learn that a blizzard has buried the Northeast. To them, the cycle of the seasons is a kind of poverty. But I think they are the ones who are deprived. Their golf year has no beginning and no end. They don't get to savor a season's two most consequential rounds:

its first and its last. For them, one year blends into the next, and they never reach a point from which they are forced to assess their golf game's progress or decline.

They also lack the concept of the "bonus day," a term for which there is no equivalent in Floridian. Where I live, bonus days first become possible in late October, when there are no pages left in the tournament calendar, and the temperature falls below freezing at night, and the water in the clubhouse bathroom has been shut off to protect the pipes. Some players simply quit at that point, content to let their golf clubs hibernate till spring, but most of my regular buddies and I break out our thermal golf gloves and our knit caps, and hang on for as long as we can.

There have been years when Bob has closed our greens before Halloween, so we know the end could come at any time. Occasionally, though, the weather takes a sudden turn for the balmy, and a predicted inch of snow falls on South Carolina instead of on us, and the thermometer at noon looks as though it got stuck in mid-September. On days like that, I drum my fingers on my desk, and try to keep my eyes from drifting to the window. Words swim on my computer screen. Then the phone rings, and I know before lifting the receiver that it's Jim or Rick or Hacker or Ray.

"Twelve-thirty?"

"Probably not. I've got a million things to do. Well, maybe, I guess. But don't wait for me."

Of course, we all show up. "Bonus day," someone inevitably

says, and we know there can't be many left. Nick, who works at the post office, rushes up to the club on his lunch break, still wearing his uniform and his black ripple-sole shoes, and he plays along for four or five holes, one eye on his wristwatch. Bill sometimes reschedules a real-estate closing.

Even if there are six or seven of us, we'll sometimes play as a single group, because who knows when we'll all have a chance to play together again? Half a dozen golfers can play eighteen holes in three and a half hours, if they pick up when they're out of the hole. We don't dawdle; by mid-November, it's hard to see a golf ball after three-thirty, and it's almost impossible after four.

Sometimes, Bob walks along with us, or even plays. The greens don't need to be mowed anymore, because they'll survive the coming winter better if they're shaggy, so he has the time. Usually, he leaves his bag in his garage and carries just his eight-iron—which he also uses as a putter, by turning it around and stroking it left-handed. Even backwards, he's probably the best putter in the club. He keeps his competitive appetite under control by focusing on making our matches come out even. If his team is ahead, he misses putts on purpose; if his team is behind, he hits shots you wouldn't believe.

In 2001, Bob kept our greens open until just past the end of the first week of December—not a record for us, but close. By that point, I was almost hoping for the end. Bonus days had become bonus weeks, then more than a bonus month. Confused dandelions had popped up in the fairways, and a big clump of forsythia near the pond on the fourth hole had begun to bloom. I was behind in my work, and so was everyone else. Our wives and children had begun to complain.

Winter finally did arrive, of course. On what would turn out to be the last bonus day of the year, Bob himself joined us, with just his eight-iron. There was a big storm in the forecast for that night, and Bob paused on every hole to clean leaves from its winter cup, a white plastic cylinder sunk into each fairway about twenty yards short of the green. That night, we knew, Bob would pull all the flags and put them in the winter cups, and that's where they would stay until spring.

After the last putt had fallen on eighteen, we all shook hands and thanked Bob for another good year. "Well," he said, "you never know. The storm might change direction overnight, and you could all be back here in the morning."

You could smell the snow in the air at that point. Still, as I drove home, my heart was brimming with irrational hope.

ABOUT THE AUTHOR

DAVID OWEN is a staff writer for *The New Yorker* and a contributing editor of *Golf Digest*, for which he writes a monthly column. His other books include *The Chosen One*, *The Making of the Masters*, *My Usual Game*, *The First National Bank of Dad*, and, most recently, *Copies in Seconds*. He lives in northwest Connecticut with his wife and their two children.